Francis Allen Ellis

Historic Photography

The City of Detroit

John Francis Ellis

Dedication

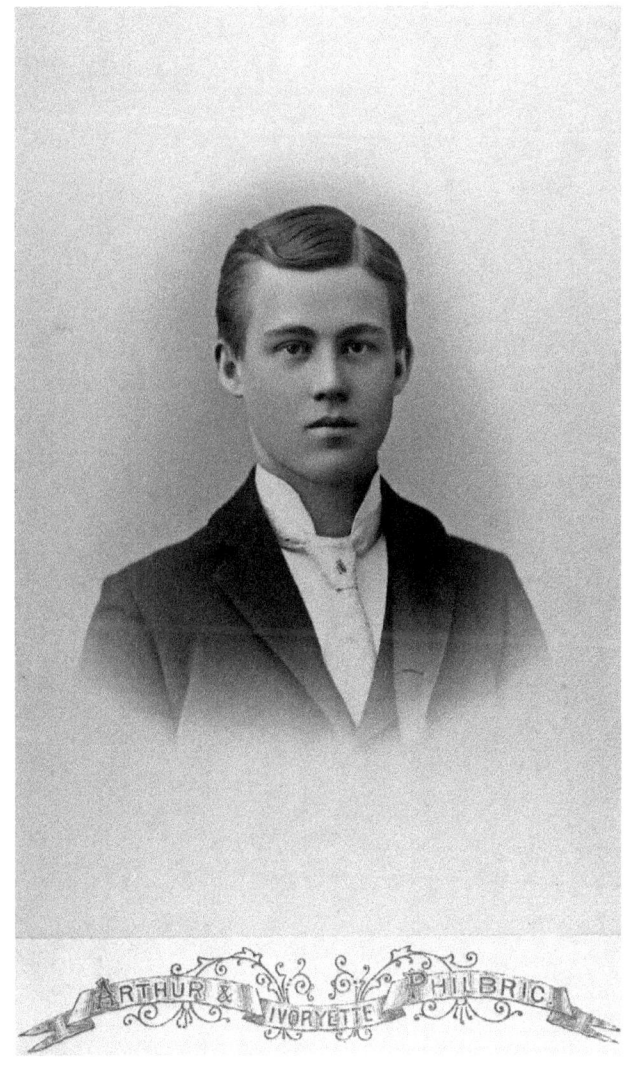

Francis Allen Ellis (1876-1950)

This collection of photographs is dedicated to my Grandfather, Francis Allen Ellis. His large collection of photographs not only left his family with a great legacy, but also provides a great legacy to anyone that has an interest in Detroit and the areas around the country that he visited.

A special thanks to cousin Bob Scott for reviewing this manuscript and offering suggestions of which I used almost every one. I also want to thank my wife Sharon and daughter Olivia for putting up with the boxes of negatives piled up on the living room floor. Last but not least, I want to thank my son Edward for his encouragement on this project and a very special thank you to my mom and dad, Kathleen and Edward Ellis, for their safekeeping, and passing on, of this family history.

Introduction

Since I was very young I have combed through my grandfathers photographs over and over again with awe. Seeing the city of Detroit and other parts of the country long gone has fascinated me. I often wished I could walk into the picture, step into the buildings and say hi to everyone I passed while checking out the environment.

My father, Edward Dale Ellis, who has compiled a tremendous genealogy database, learned to process film and prints from his father, and in turn, my father taught me. The first thing I did when I bought a house with a basement was build my own darkroom and begin printing his negatives and reproducing the photographs that no longer had negatives. Unfortunately my Grandfather died the year before I was born and I never had the opportunity to go on a shoot with him.

Because many of the old glass plate negatives that were now in my possession had begun to deteriorate, I contacted Kodak and the Smithsonian archivists to learn how to clean and protect them. They both were extremely helpful and the plates are now stored properly. It is sad that Kodak no longer has an expert to answer questions. I often wonder if these photographs would have survived if they were shot with modern digital cameras. I'm still trying to figure out how to store my photographs shot with a digital camera and have them survive the next hundred years. My current thinking is to shoot important pictures with black and white film, load the exposed film in the developing tank in a changing bag, process and then scan them.

I hope you enjoy this small collection. In total he shot hundreds and hundreds if not thousands of photographs of which I have the remainder. It is a very long and slow process, but I am cataloging them and will publish those of interest as I go through them.

This is the first in what will become a series of photo books containing the photographs taken by my grandfather. He carried his camera with him as he traveled and photographed the cities and towns as they were, bringing us a rich, photographic journey back in time. After this collection I plan to publish photos of Newbury, Vermont in 1917, The Chicago Worlds Fair, early Macomb County, as well as Detroit Shipping and Shipbuilding. A friend of mine and I were also lucky enough to be carrying Kodak 126 cameras when the rock group, The Who, first played the Grande Ball Room and I will publish them as well.

I have created the *Francis Allen Ellis - Historic Photographs* blog at **http://faellis.wordpress.com** so that I can post photographs and information can be shared. I hope that unknown buildings and locations can be identified and families may be able to identify relatives in some of the photographs.

John Francis Ellis
Grandson to **Francis Allen Ellis**

History

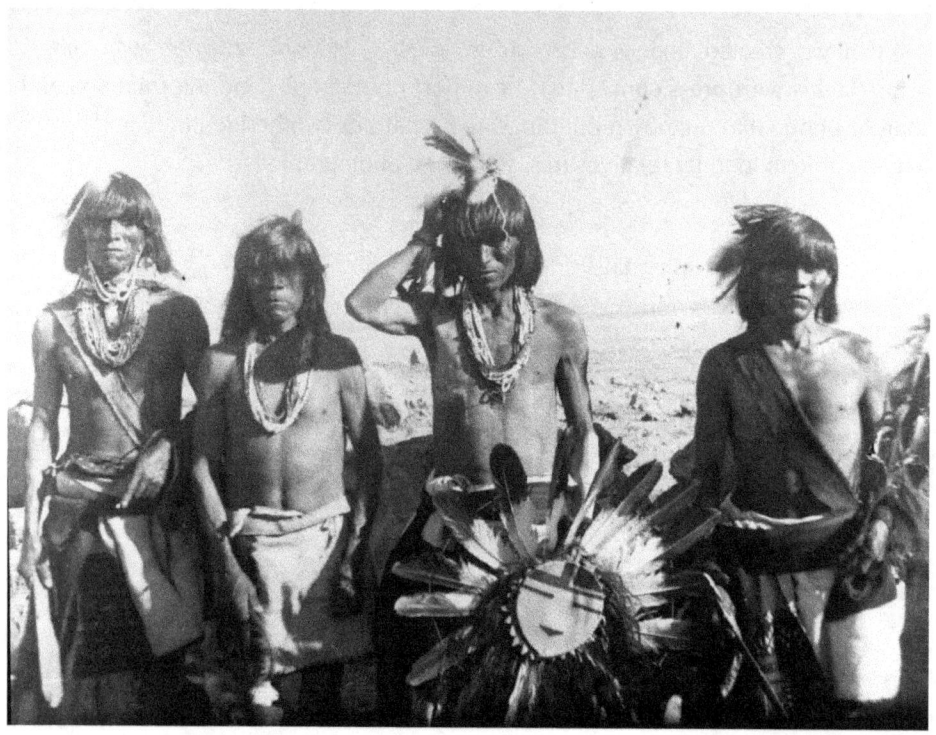

Francis Allen Ellis is a 9th generation American. He is a direct descendant of Lt. John Ellis of Sandwich, Massachusetts who was killed during the King Phillips War. His father, George Abbott Ellis, a veteran of the American Civil War was a member of the 16th Vermont Volunteer Infantry. George married Emma Newell Gould in 1872 at Brattleboro, Vermont and moved to Mahwah, New Jersey. It is in Mahwah where Francis was born on September 1, 1876. At about the age of one, Francis found himself living in Detroit where his father moved with his family to continue his trade as a machinist.

Sometime after the death of his father in 1896, Francis was invited to learn the art of developing photographs by a family friend named Robert Kern in 1896/1897. The family oral history says that this was probably to help keep his mind occupied after the early death of his father. He printed several photos his friend took of Native Americans on a trip he had taken to Arizona. These prints were placed in a photo album that was passed on to me by my father.

The Native American photo shown is scanned directly from one of the prints that he made from Roberts negatives. The note in his photo album says, "Indian pictures from Robert Kern's negatives in Arizona."

I've tried to find a reference for Robert Kern in online historical records but have not found anything concrete. More of these prints will be published in future volumes and I hope that I can find out who Robert Kerns was before then.

It was right after this printing experience that Francis began taking photographs. His first prints are dated 1897 and shot on 4X5 inch glass plates. He was twenty years old. In 1904 he married Kathryn Belle Giddings of Macomb Township. Kathryn added her own family legacy as an artist. She created wonderful hand painted china and oil paintings that hang in homes all across the country.

The earliest negatives are on 4X5 inch glass plates. He later began shooting with 5X7 inch glass plates then moved to 5X7 inch film. He eventually began using 4X5 inch film and other odd size large format film and eventually used various medium format films, especially 6X9 cm.

At some point Francis donated many of his glass plates to the Burton Historical collection in the Detroit Public Library. In 1952 my father donated another batch of them. I have seen them in books and leaflets without credit to him. The Burton Historical Collection did not record the name of the photographer of the donated plates and photos during that time period which has made it difficult to discover any negatives that I may not have prints of. Thankfully, the Burton Historical Collection has begun digitizing their collection and putting them on-line, I have been able to match many of them in this book with those in their collection. I will be meeting with The Burton Historical Collection in the near future so that his name can be added to the record and I can share photo information from my grandfathers notes.

Throughout his life, Francis photographed his family and the places he visited until his death on Christmas Eve 1950.

The following is an excerpt from the 1922 publication, "The City of Detroit, Michigan, 1701-1922, Volume 5, page 433":

"Francis A. Ellis. In business circles of Detroit, Francis A. Ellis is well known as Advertising manager and welfare officer of the Russell Wheel & Foundry Company, (Chene St. and Belt Line Crossing, Detroit) one of the oldest and most substantial manufacturing enterprises of the city, with which he has been identified for a period of twenty-seven years, entering the employ of the firm in a humble capacity and advancing with the development of the business until he now occupies a position of trust and responsibility. A native of New Jersey, he was born at Mahwah on the 1st of September, 1876, his parents being George A. and Emma N. (Gould) Ellis, the former a native of Rindge, New Hampshire, while the latter was born at Newbury, Vermont. They were married in the Green Mountain state and in 1877 took up their residence in Detroit, where the father continued to follow the machinist's trade, with which he had previously been connected in various manufacturing centers in the east. He passed away in this city in 1896. The mother is still residing here. In their family were three children: Mrs. Herbert J. Conn, whose husband is the president of the Peninsular Screw Company of Detroit; Mrs. Hugh McNeal, who is the wife of the president of the Detroit Metal & Steel Works; and Francis A., of this review. Mr. Ellis acquired his education in the grammar and high schools of Detroit and in 1894, when eighteen years of age, he secured the position of office boy with the Russell Wheel & Foundry Company. He bent every energy toward learning the business, faithfully and efficiently performing each task assigned him, and his efforts were rewarded by promotion from one position to another of greater responsibility until he was made advertising manager in 1909, while in the same year he was also appointed welfare manager. Through his enterprising and aggressive business methods the sales of the company have been greatly augmented and in his capacity as welfare officer he is capably looking after the interest of several hundred employees, securing their cooperation and efficiency in the operation of the plant, which is one of the largest of Detroit's industries. In this city, on the 27th of June 1904, Mr. Ellis was united in marriage to Miss Kathryn B. Giddings, a daughter of Mr. and Mrs. T. M. Giddings, well known residents of Macomb County, Michigan.

Mr. Ellis gives his political allegiance to the republican party and is a member of the Presbyterian Church of Royal Oak, where the residence of the family is maintained. He is chairman of the Foundry-men's Division of the Employers' Association and is a member of the Adcraft Club, Order of Odd Fellow. He is a man whom to know is to esteem and honor. He has eagerly grasped every opportunity which has come his way and step by step has advanced. His career has been actuated by a spirit of progress and he deserves classification with the self-made men and valued citizens of Detroit, in which city practically his entire life has been spent."

The Home Of Francis Allen Ellis

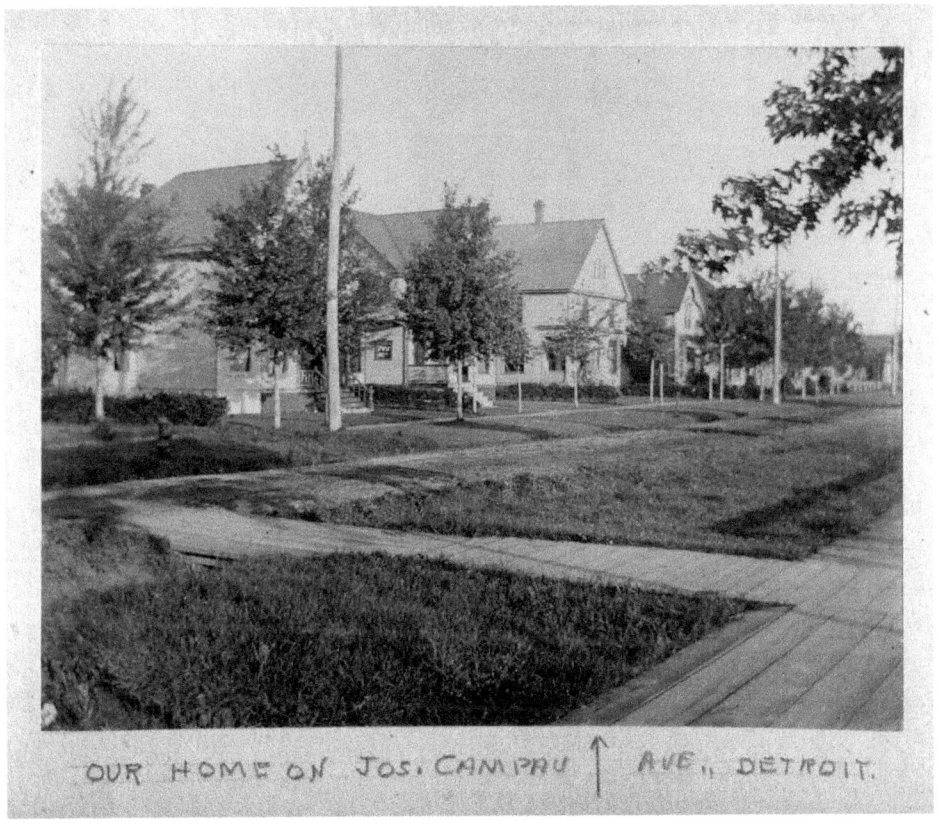

OUR HOME ON JOS. CAMPAU ↑ AVE., DETROIT.

This is a scanned page from a photo book given to his mother for Christmas 1898. It shows the home he lived in with his family at 1209 Joseph Campau, Detroit. The area where this house was appears to have been redeveloped and none of these homes exists today.

The City Of Detroit

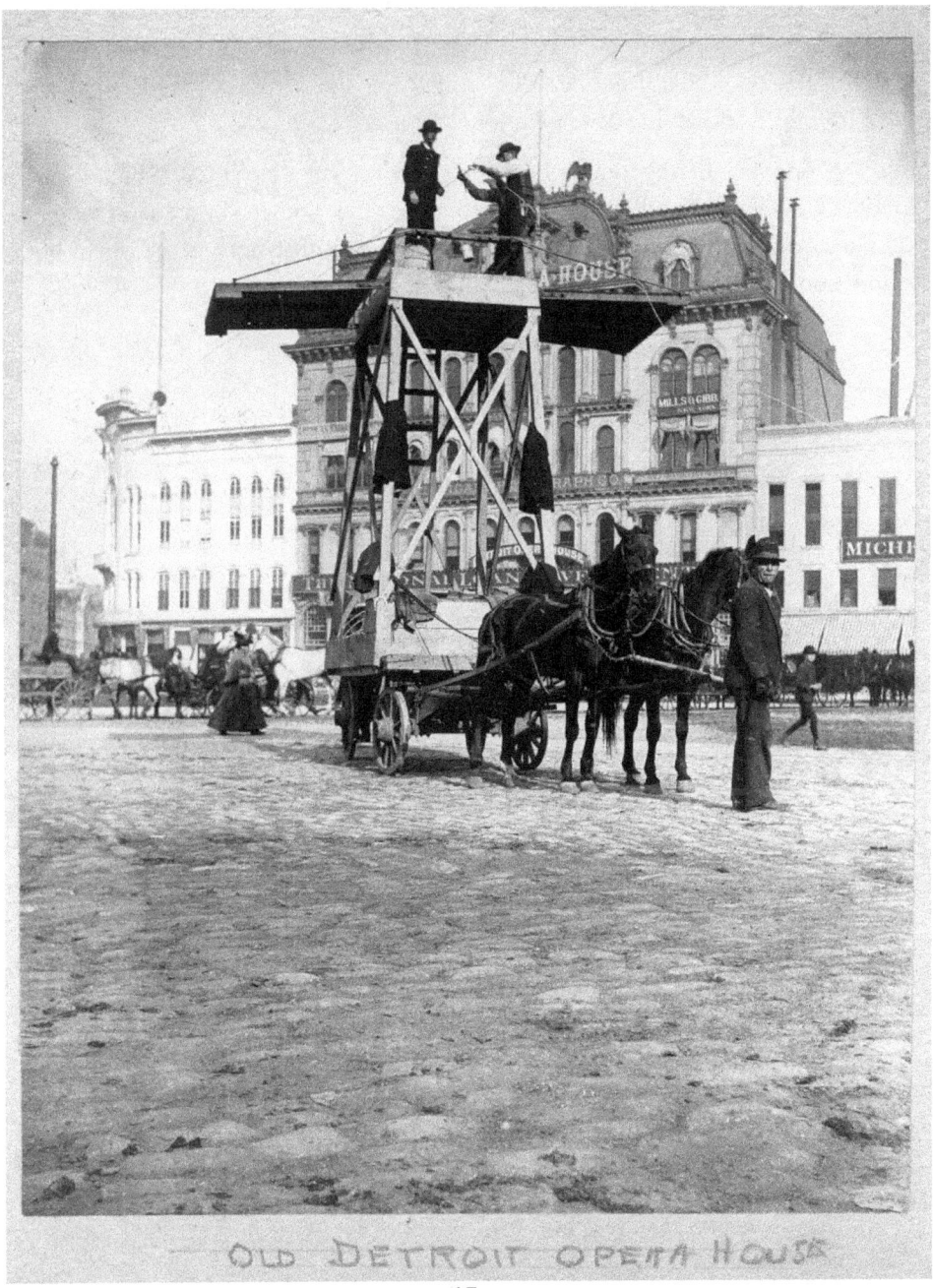

OLD DETROIT OPERA HOUSE

From another photo scanned from the 1898 Christmas photo book given to his mother, a trolley repair wagon stands in front of the old Detroit Opera House with workers making a repair on the overhead cables. This photo was taken before fire destroyed it on October 7, 1897.

The opening of the opera house took place on March 29, 1869. It was modeled after the pavilions that surrounded the Louvre in Paris, France by Architect Mortimer L. Smith. J. L. Hudson opened his first store in the opera house before constructing his own building by the same architect.

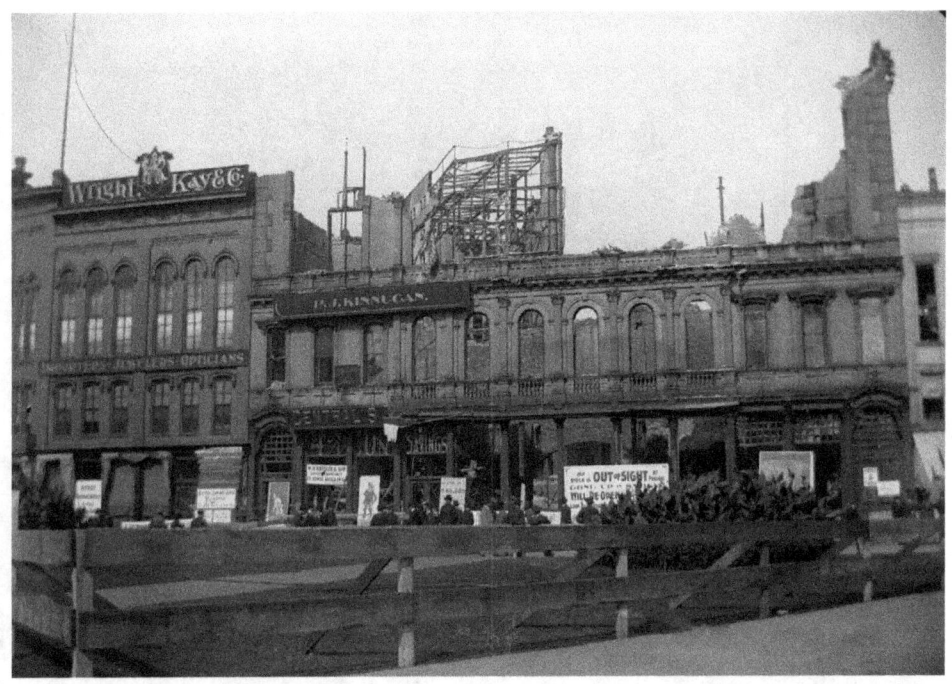

The remains of the Detroit Opera house lay vacant after the fire in 1897. Signs direct customers to new locations where shops from inside the building have relocated.

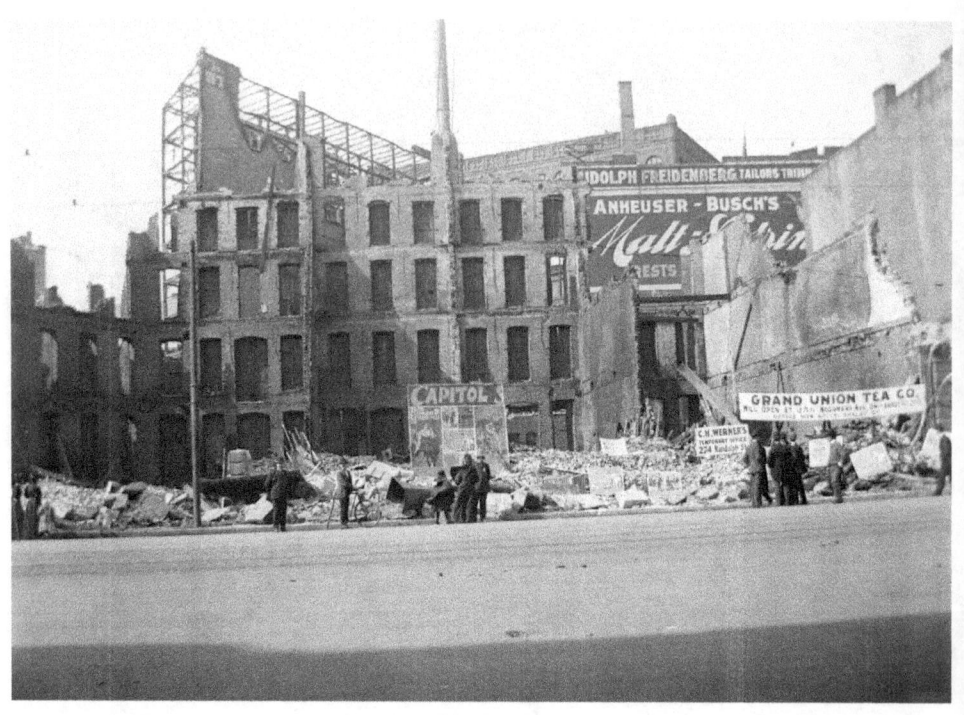

Another view of the burned out Detroit Opera House with an Anheuser-Busch sign still intact on the side of the building.

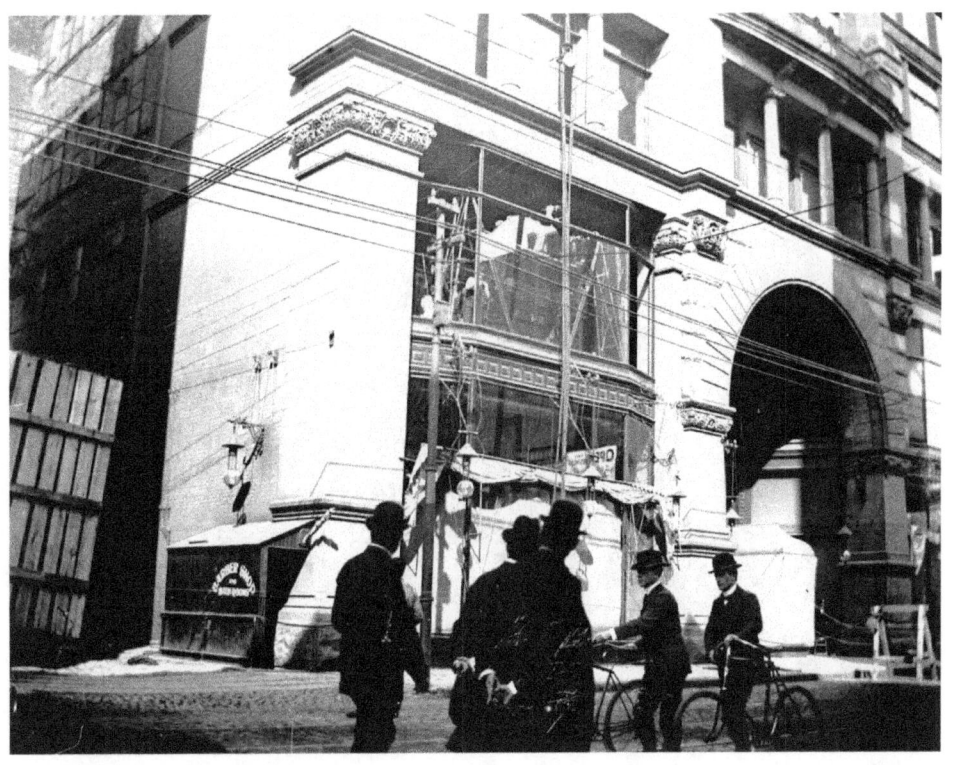

Bystanders gaze toward a window cracked from the heat of the 1897 Opera House fire at the J. L. Hudson store.

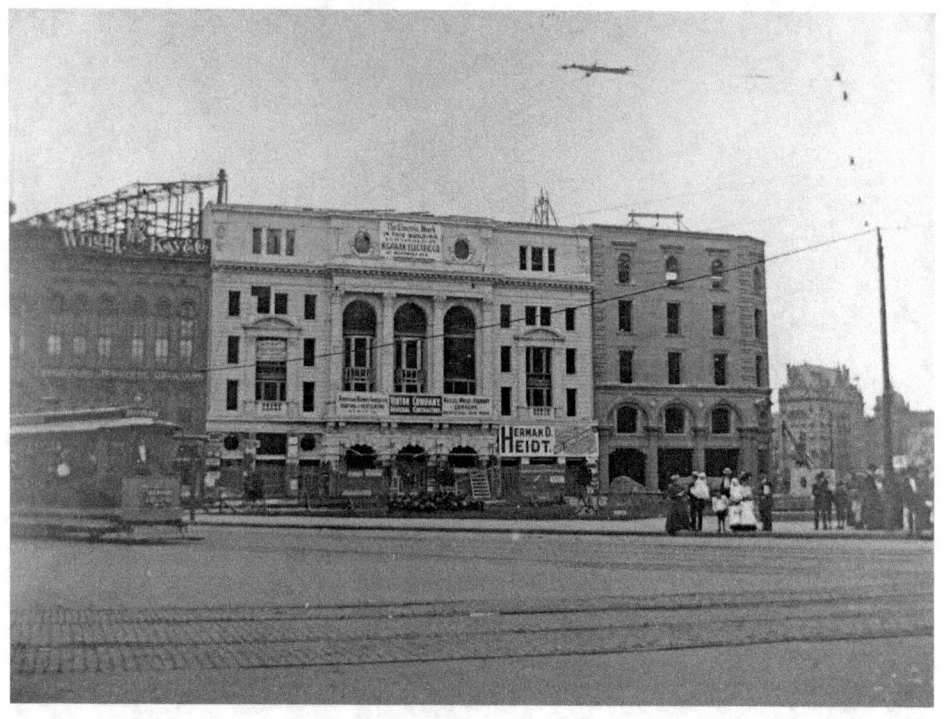

The new Detroit Opera House shown here was rebuilt on the same site and reopened on Sept 12, 1898. This photo was shot during the reconstruction.

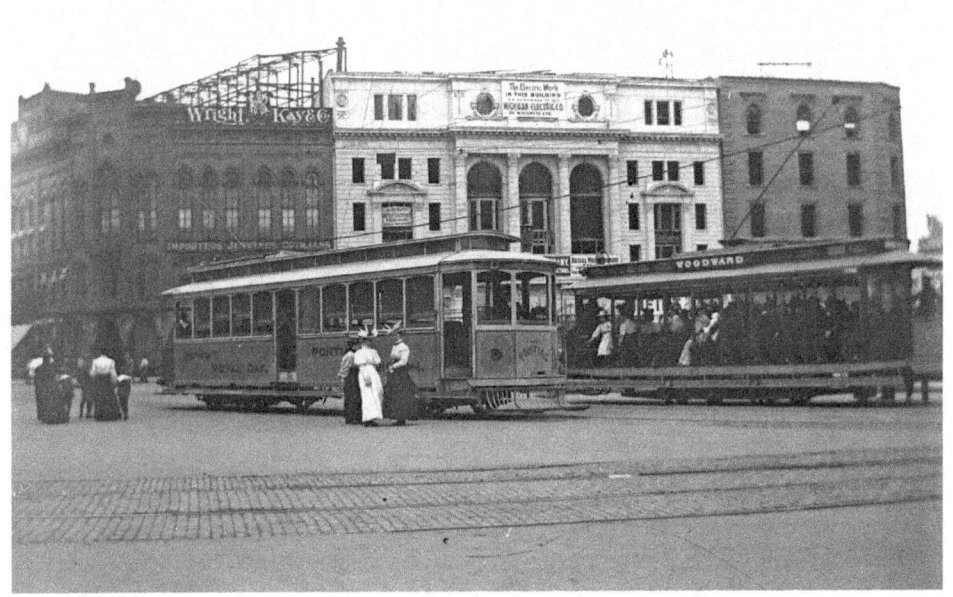

Another view of the Detroit Opera House during the rebuilding in 1897/98 shows Oakland Railway suburban rail cars. The Woodward car is a summer car. You can read Detroit, Royal Oak and Pontiac on the side of the car on the left.

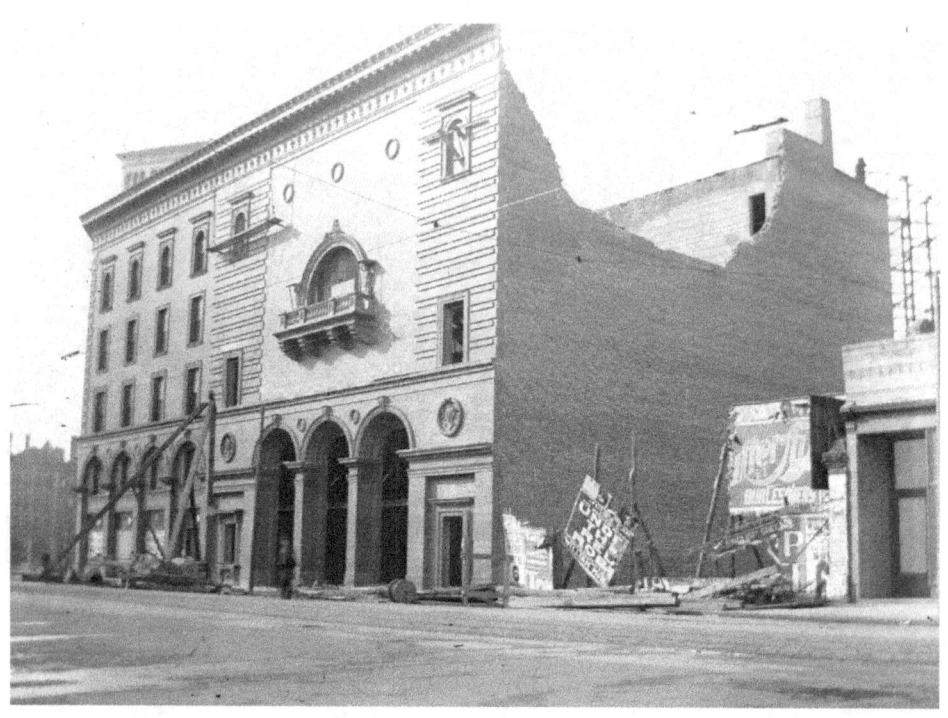

I've never been able to identify this damaged building. There were no notes left with it but I continue to hope to find some reference or another photo of it. The steel framework on the right looks as though it could be part of the structure from the burned out Detroit Opera House. There was a lot of collateral damage from the fire and this building may have been one of the casualties.

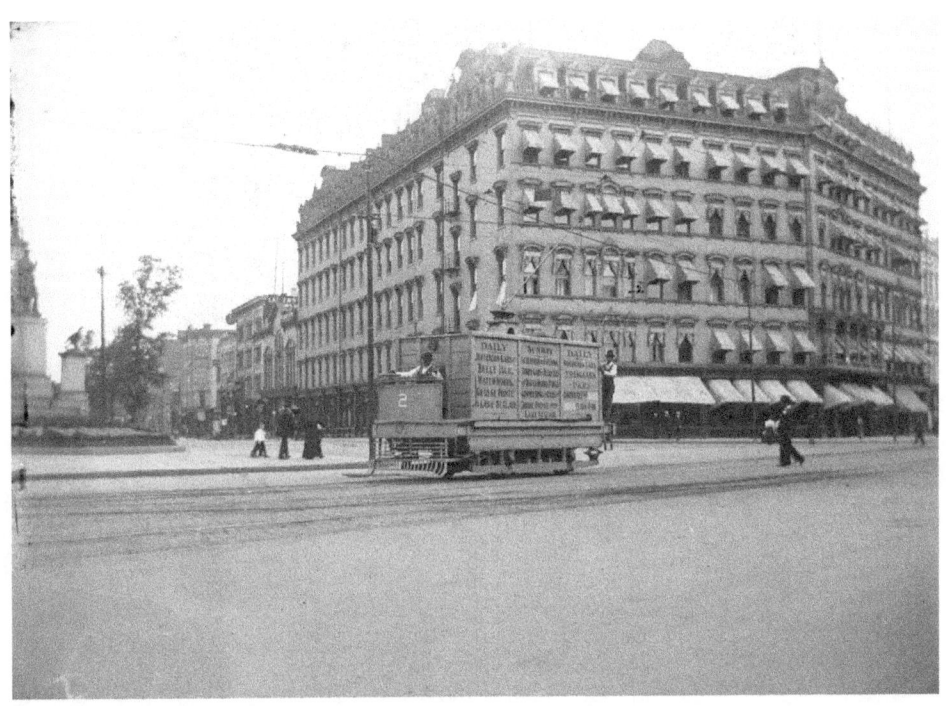

A trolley sprinkler car moves through Campus Martius. These cars were used to keep dust down during the summer months.

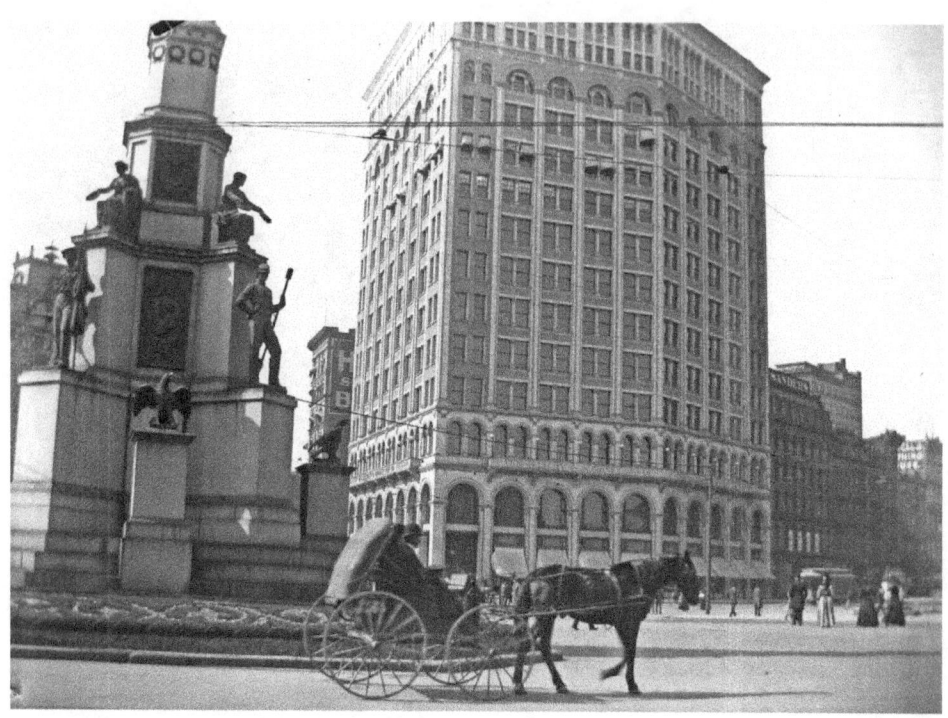

The Soldiers and Sailors Monument at Campus Martius can be seen as a horse and buggy stroll past it. It was unveiled April 9, 1872 to a crowd of about 25,000 people and was one of the first monuments to honor Civil War veterans anywhere in the US. It is one of the oldest public art pieces in Detroit and was moved 125 feet directly south of this location and given a new base in 2003. I believe that the monument is the only structure in this photo that still exists.

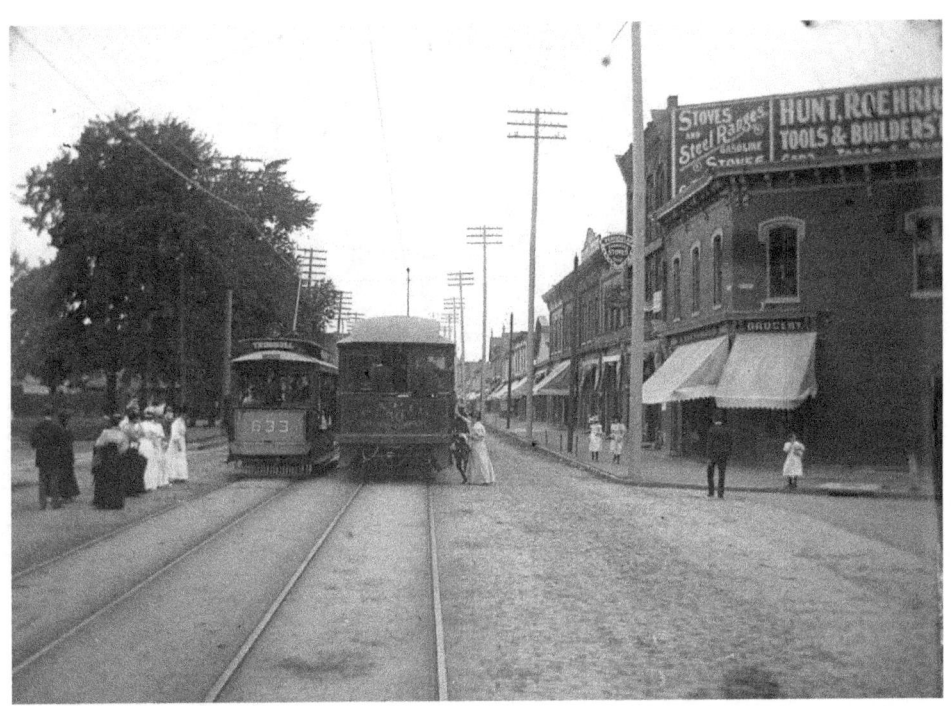

This photo of Gratiot at the corner of Saint Aubin in 1897 is one of his early photographs and has always been one of my favorites. The building locations are now an empty lot. In my quest to verify his notes on the location, I did a search for B. Youngblood Grocery as seen on the corner store sign. I was able to find a Bernard Youngblood who had, "Re-entered the grocery and feed trades in 1889. In 1899 he erected a new building on St. Aubin at the corner Hendricks." Hendricks is a street that runs directly behind the store. It is now an empty abandoned street leading me to the conclusion that he probably built a new store directly behind this one.

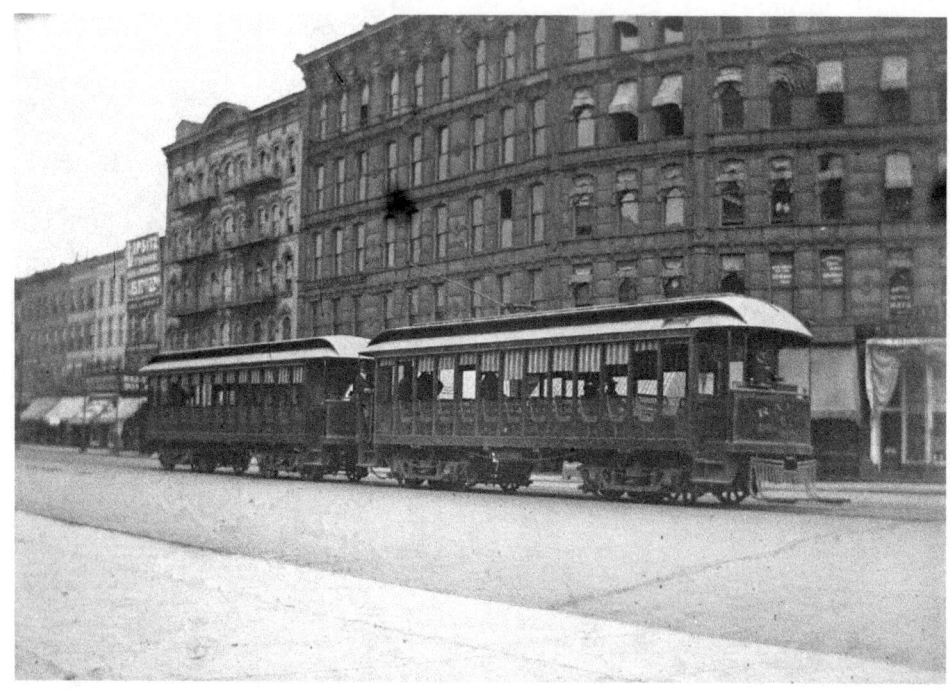

A pair of Rapid City summer cars stop in front of an unidentified building. Mt. Clemens Fast Line can be seen printed on the side of the car in front.

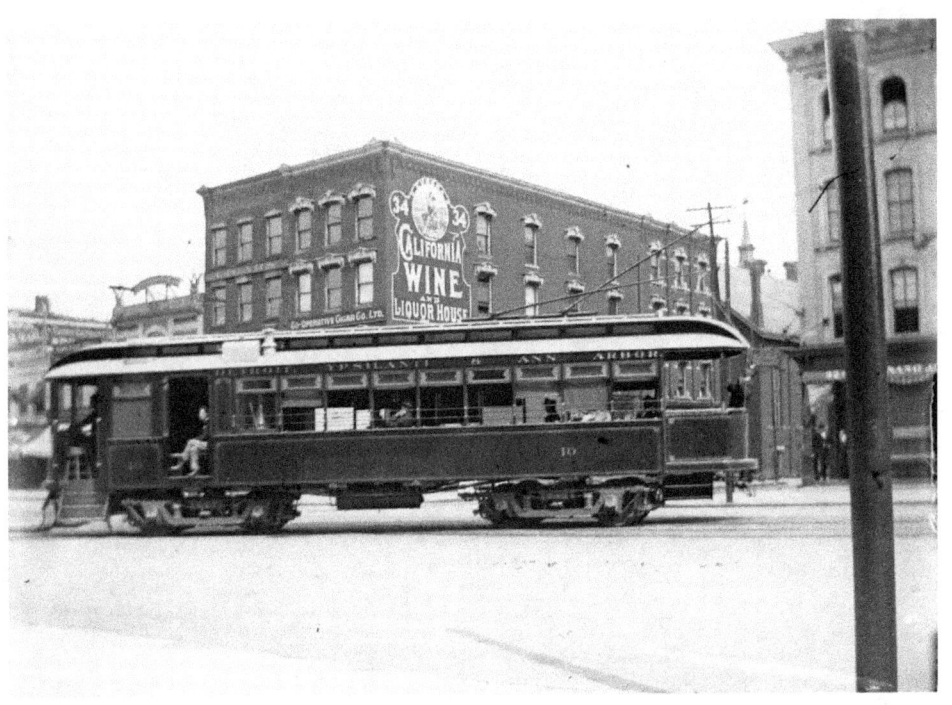

A Detroit-Ypsilanti-Ann Arbor car stops on its route with the California Wine and Liquor House sign in the background.

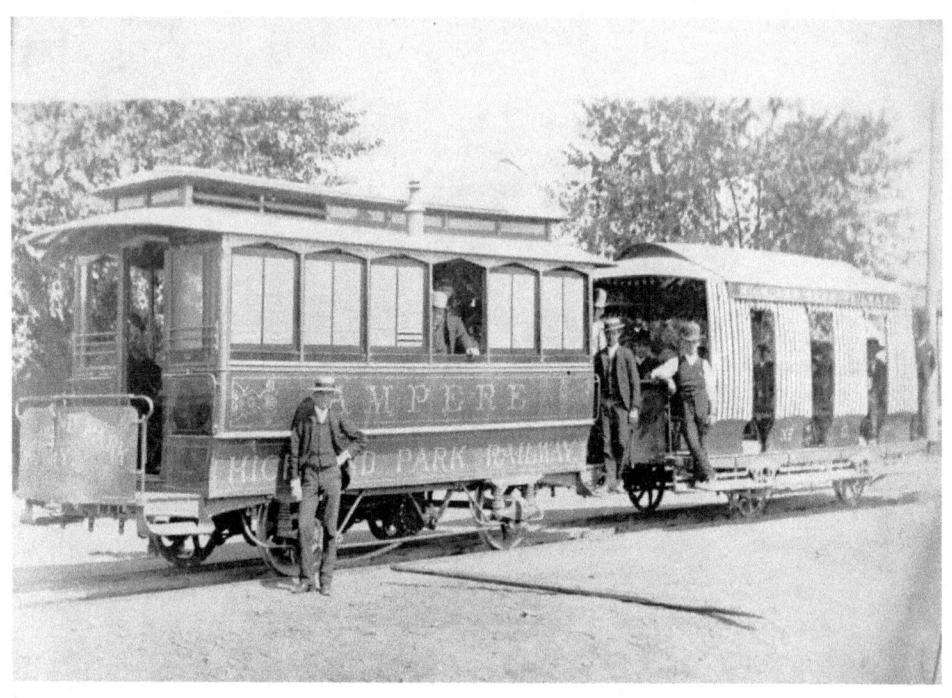

Several men pose for a photograph on these Highland Park railway cars at an unknown location.

August 25, 1898
Business Men's Parade/Jubilee
Peace Parade
Downtown Detroit

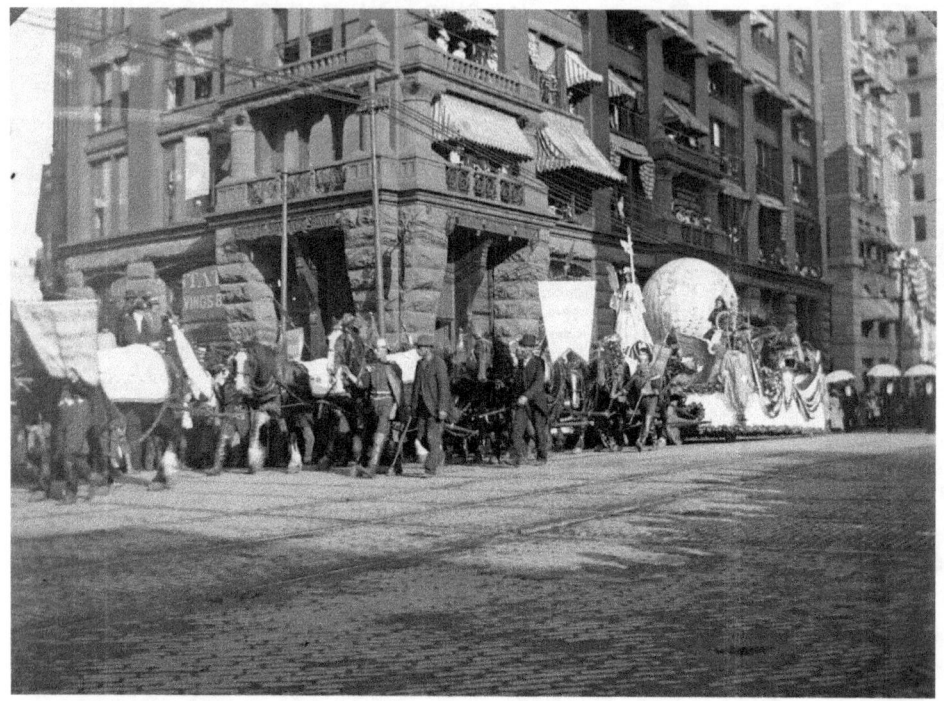

The Jubilee peace float moves down the street at Griswold and Fort Street pulled by a team of horses. The Business Men's Parade took place in Detroit on August 25, 1898. The building in the background is the Hammond building which was torn down in 1956 and replaced by The National Bank of Detroit building.

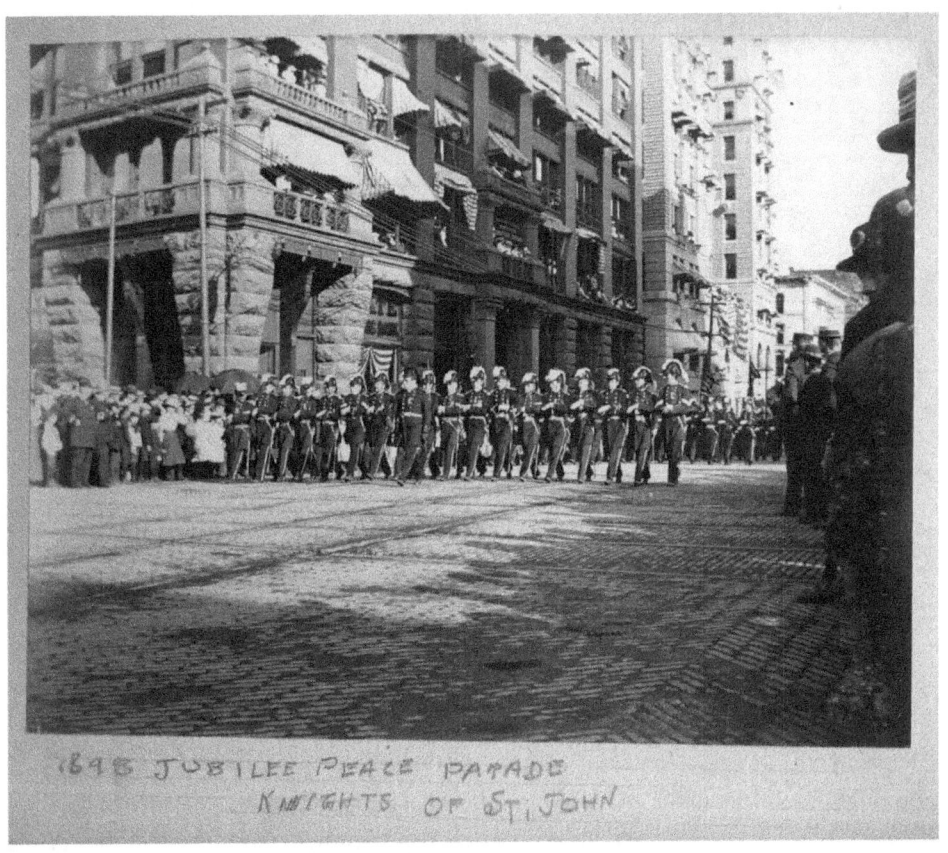

The Knights of St. John pass by the Hammond building in review during the 1898 Business Men's Parade.

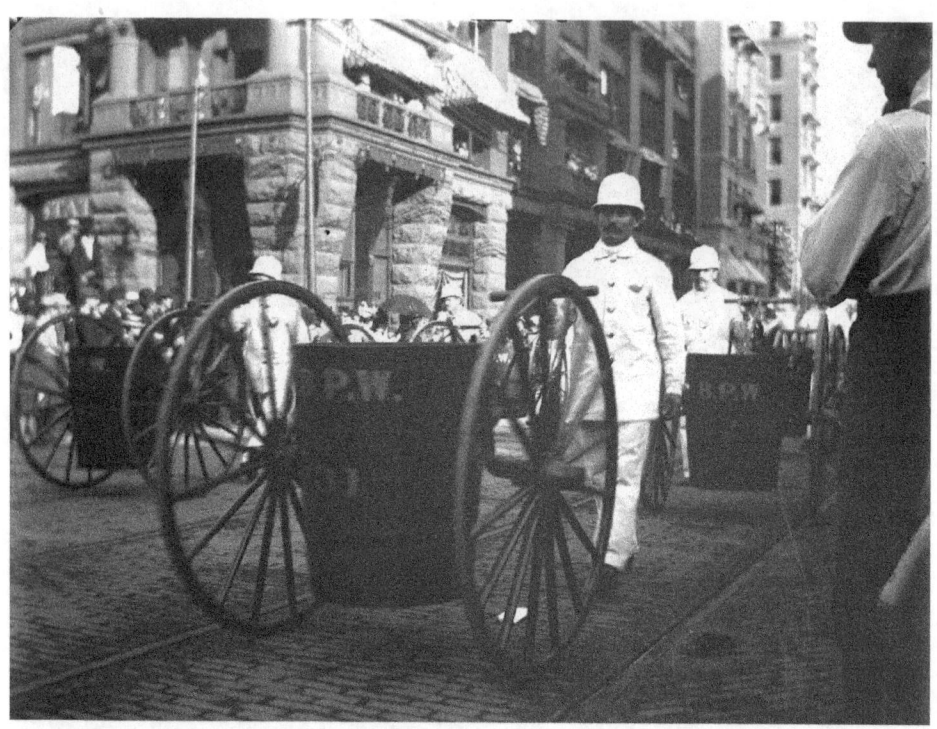

Shown in this photograph is Moreland's White Wings. D. W. H. Moreland was appointed Commissioner of Public Works in Detroit in 1896. He started a *keep Detroit clean* system immediately after his appointment and created the White Wings. The White Wings were responsible for keeping the areas around the paved streets and alleys in the center of the city and the arteries feeding them clean. Moreland was also known for posting the first *"Don't Spit"* signs around the city.

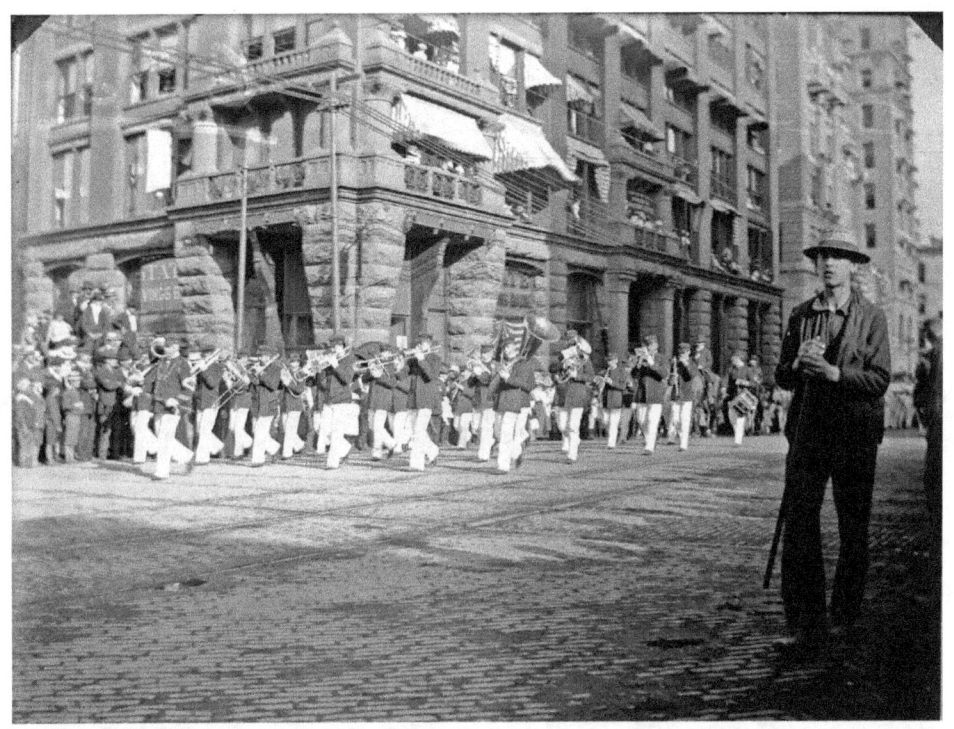

This band is identified as Schremer's band. I have been unable to find out who they were and would welcome any information anyone has.

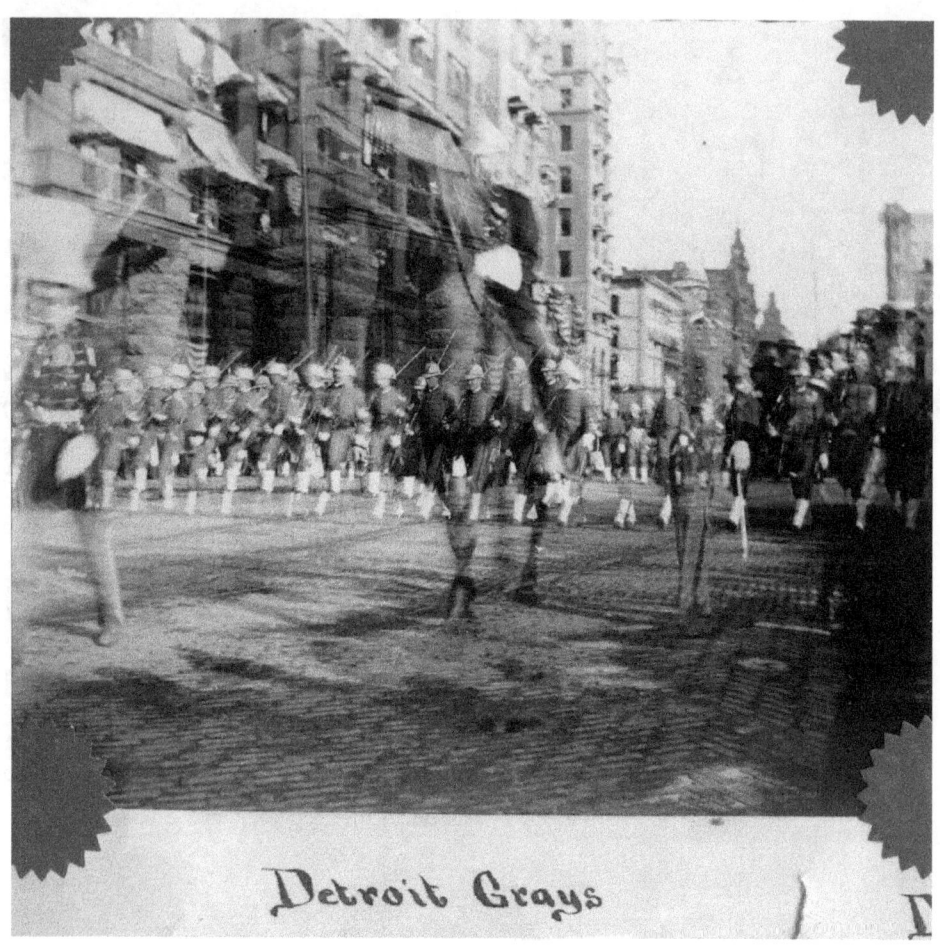

The Detroit Grays photo is a double exposure. I have found several double exposures in his collection. Some of them were intentional but my guess is that this one is an accident. It is fitting that the ghostly rider appears to be fading off into history.

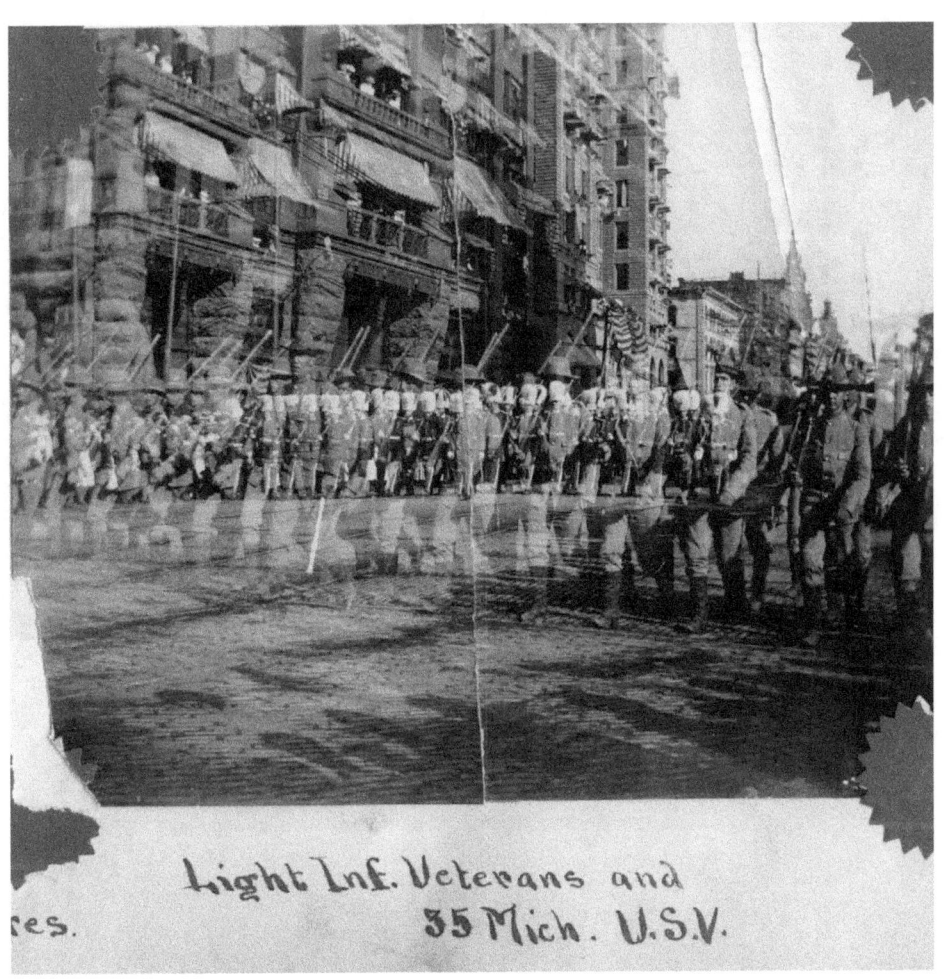

Light Inf. Veterans and
35 Mich. U.S.V.

This is another double exposure that is probably an accident. The Light Infantry Veterans and the 35th Michigan United States Volunteers fade into the past here as well.

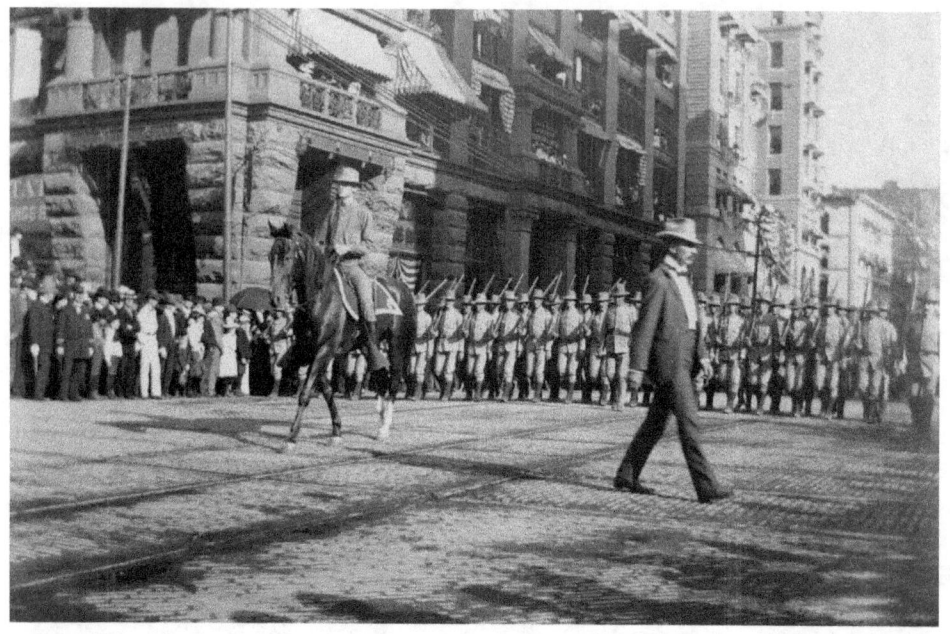

The 35th Michigan United States Volunteers March past the Hammond Building while a man crosses the street in front of them.

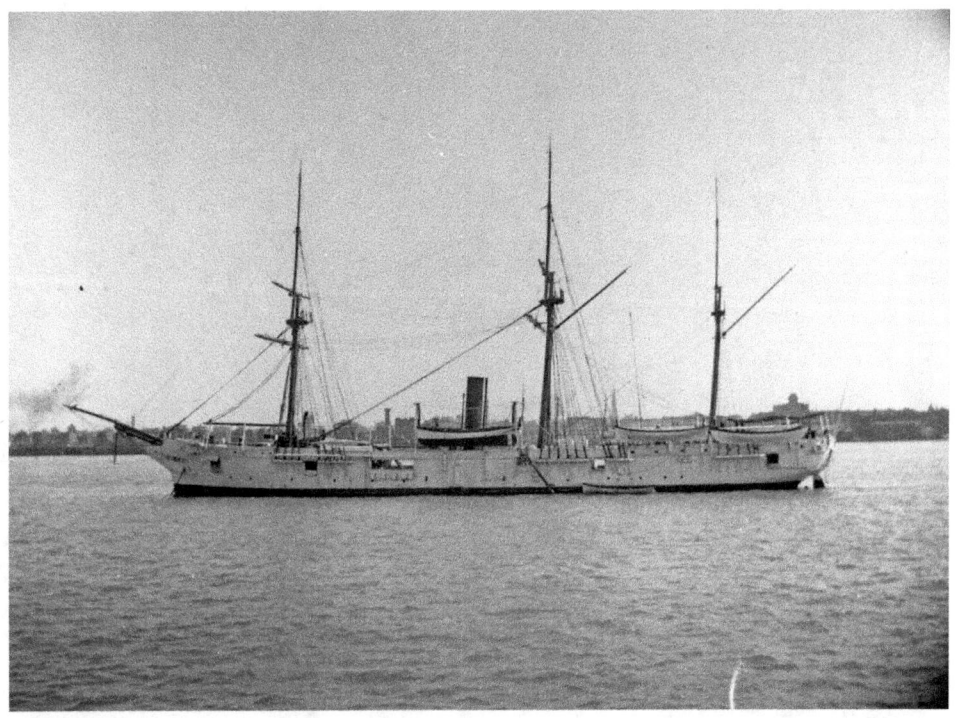

Although there is another photo from the rear of this ship, its identity is not known. My grandfather's note just says, "Ship used in Spanish American War".

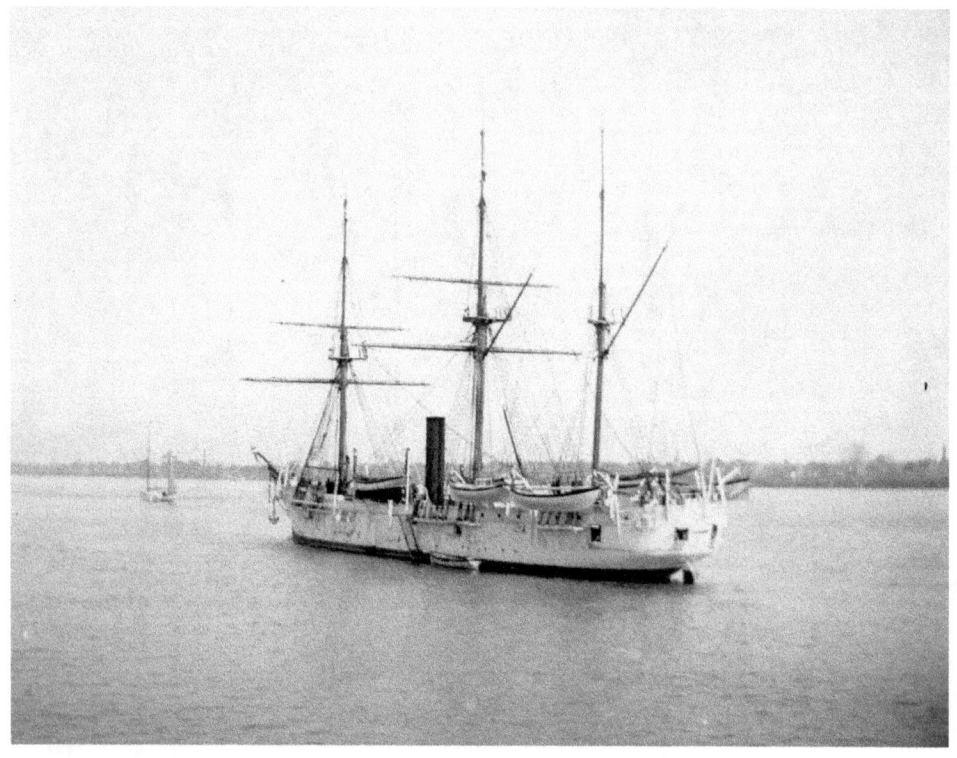

Another view of the Spanish American warship.

Belle Isle

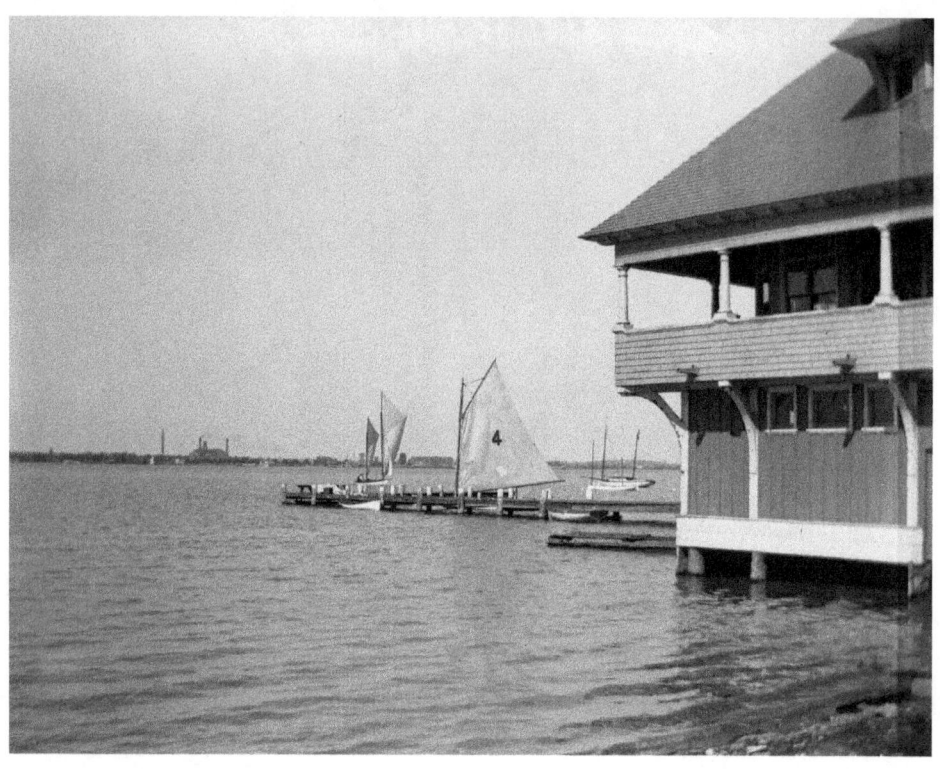

The Detroit Yacht Club was founded in 1868. The clubhouse is shown as it was in the late 1890's.

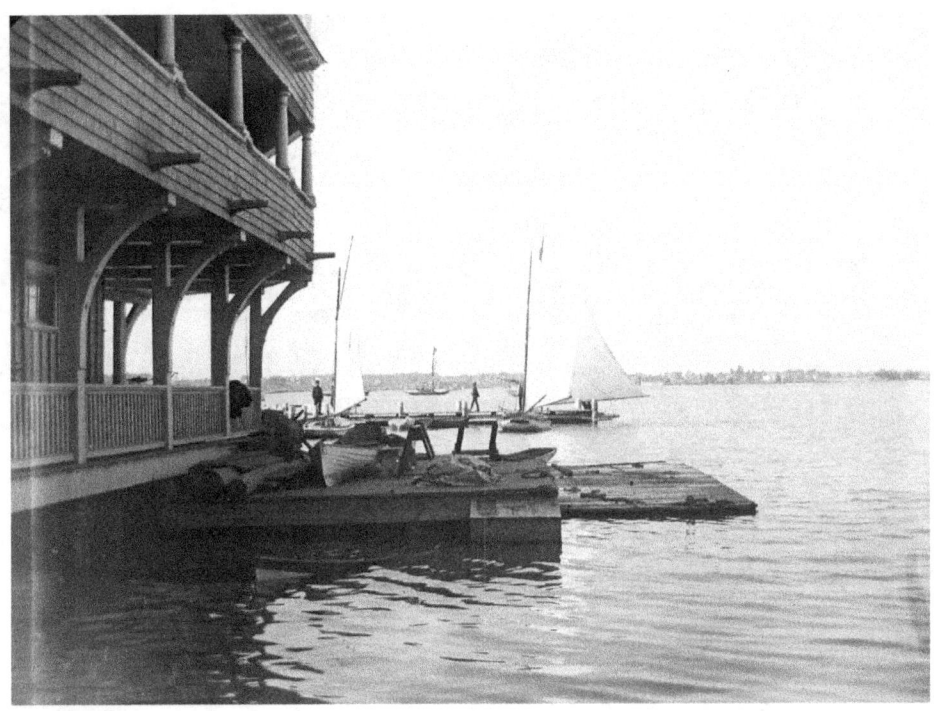

This is a view under the veranda of the Detroit Yacht Club in the late 1890's. Sailboats appear ready to get underway.

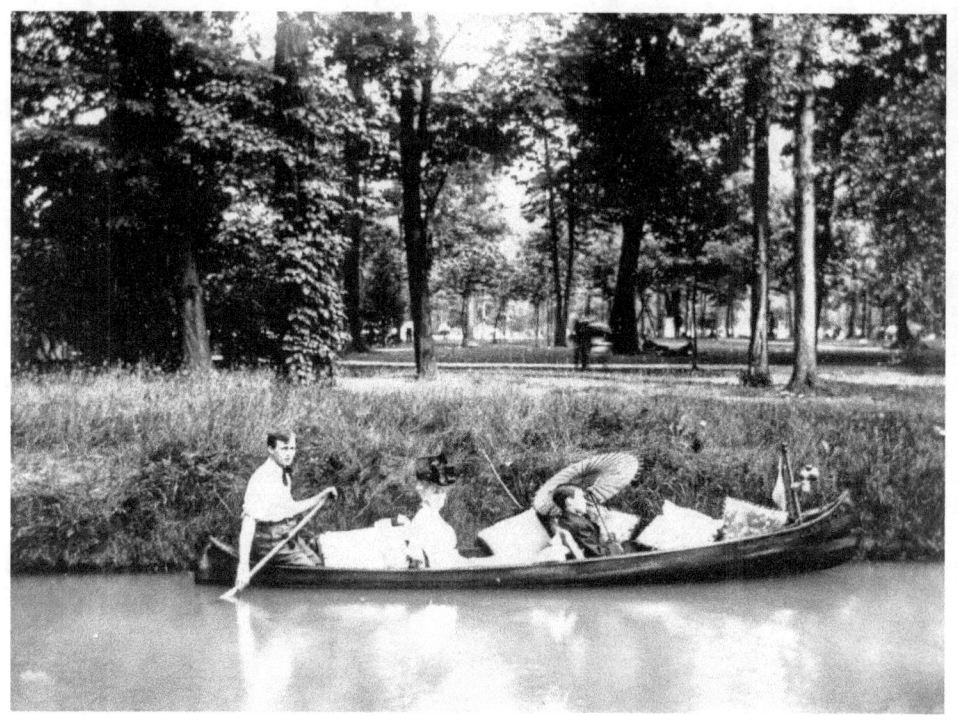

Francis with his mother and cousin Rollin MacNeil, canoeing the canals at Belle Isle.

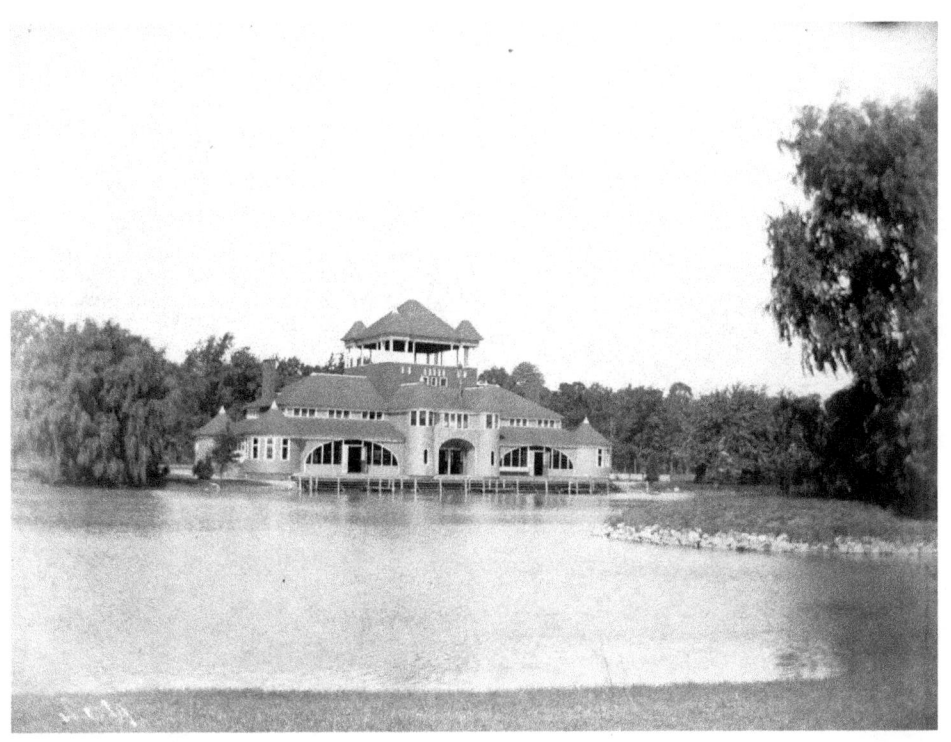

The old Belle Isle Skating Pavilion stands across the canal in the late 1890's.

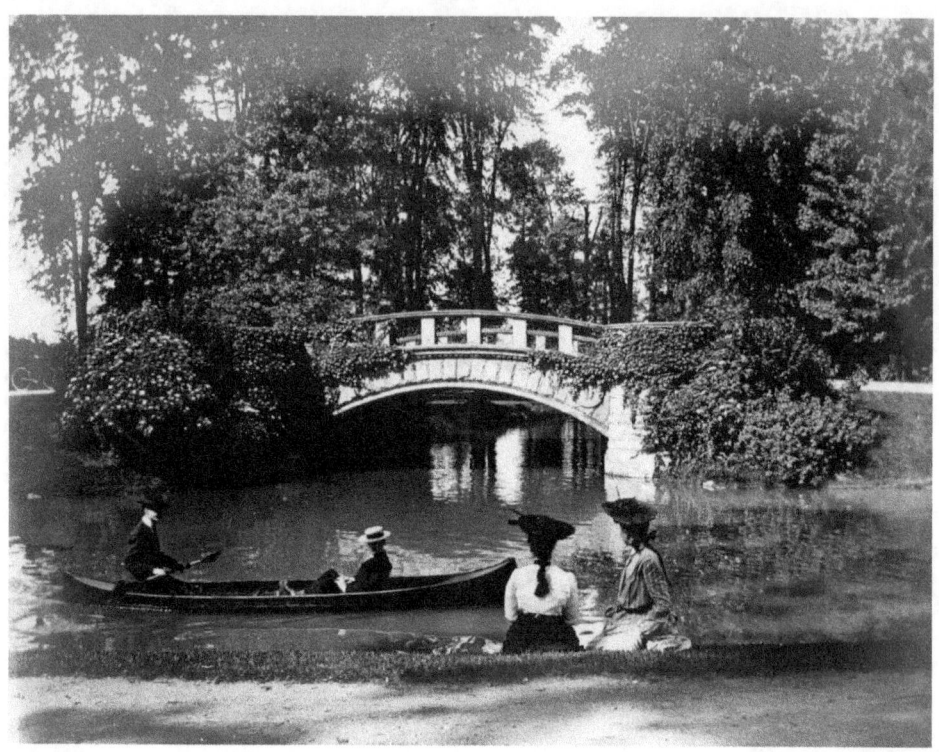

This turn of the century photograph shows my Grandmother, Kathryn Belle (Giddings) Ellis and Great Grandmother, Emma Newell (Gould) Ellis watching a canoe row by. My music CD, *Having Fun*, released in 2002, used this photo for the CD cover.

Palmer Park

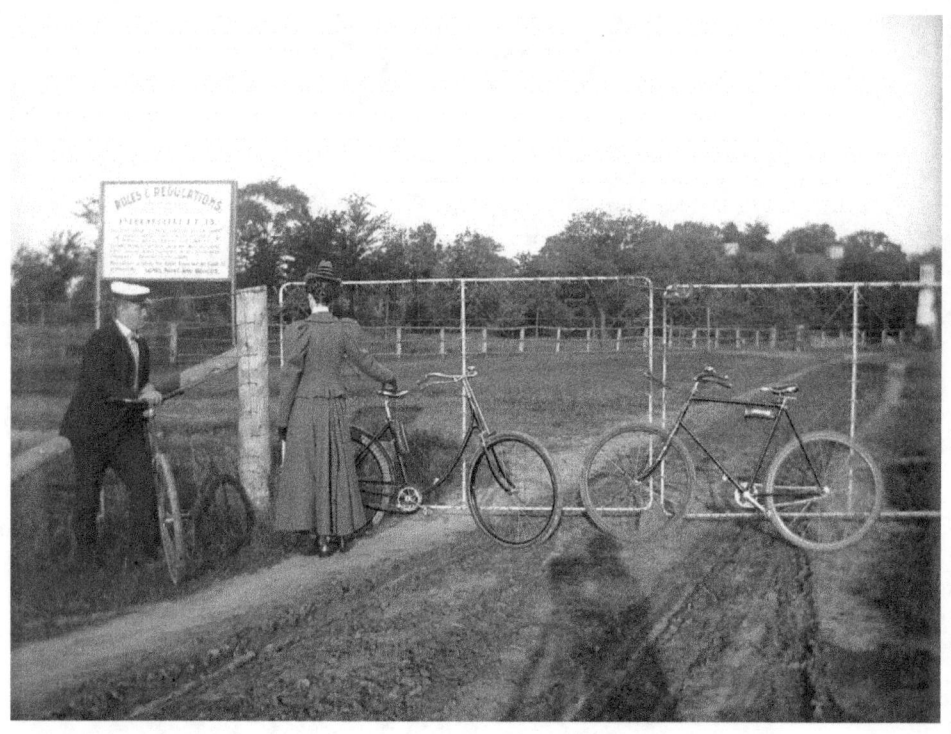

With the gate closed, bicyclers await the opening of the park. The shadow of Francis with his camera on the tripod can be seen in front and the Palmer Park lighthouse can be seen on the right.

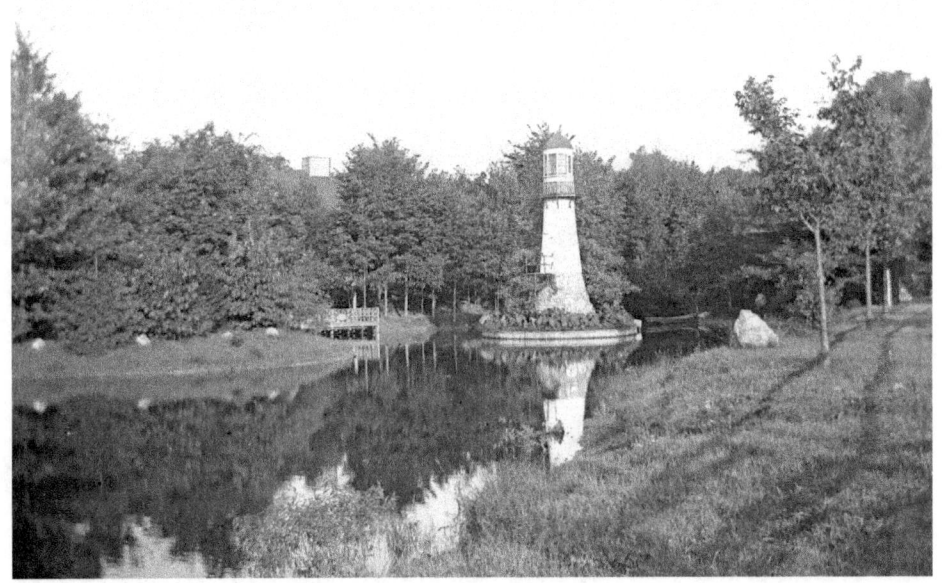

The lighthouse can still be seen at Palmer Park today. However it is in disrepair and is a far less inviting place to visit than it was when this photograph was taken.

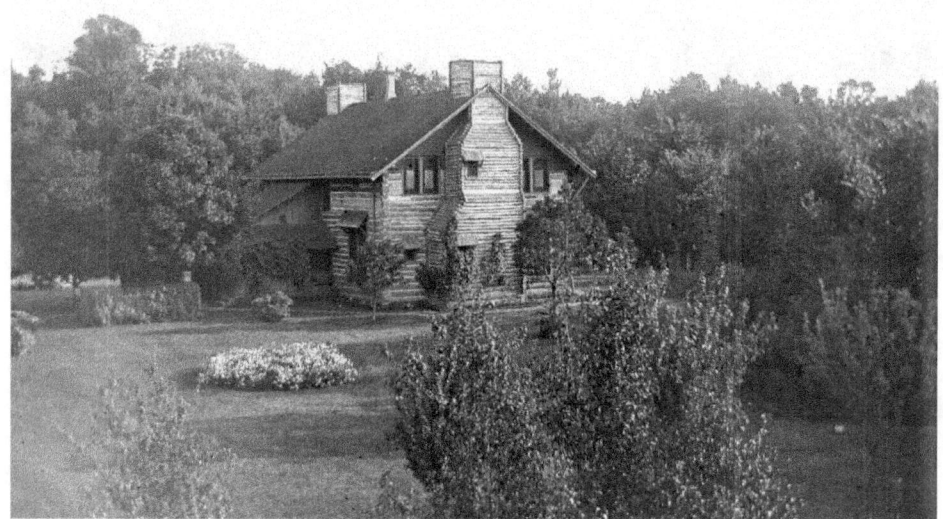

The Palmer Park log cabin is also still standing and is maintained, but rarely open to the public. I remember visiting Palmer Park when I was young and feeding the birds in the lake. You could also take horse and buggy rides through the park.

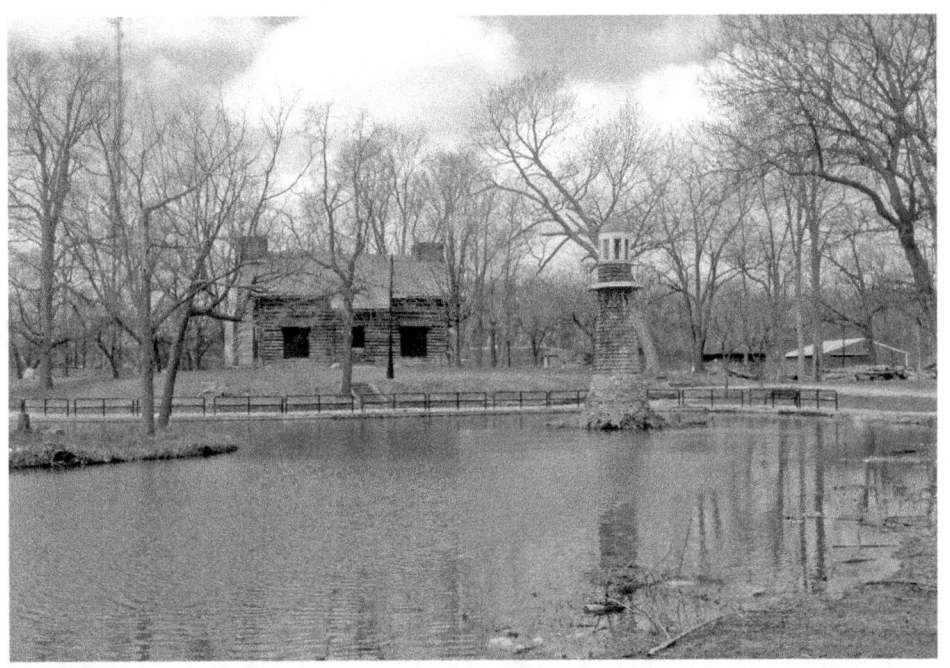

On April 21, 2013 I paid a visit to Palmer Park and captured the log cabin and lighthouse with my phone camera as they stand today. The inviting gardens are no more and the cabin and lighthouse sit in disrepair. It's too bad that someone with the resources doesn't restore the park to its former glory.

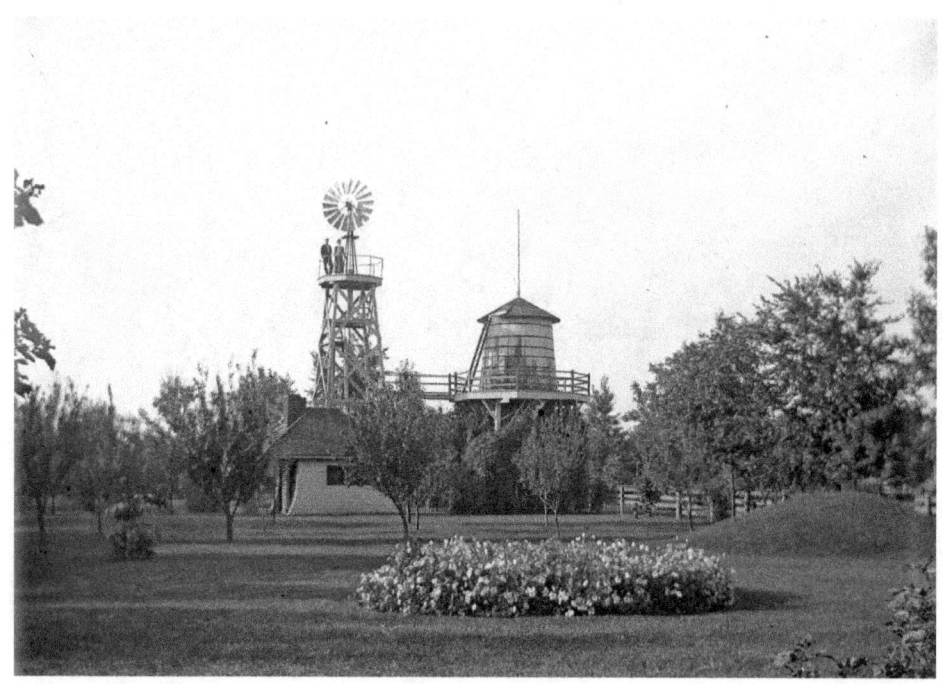

The windmill and the water tower are no longer standing. I don't remember seeing them when I was young, so they have probably been gone for a very long time.

Detroit Water Works

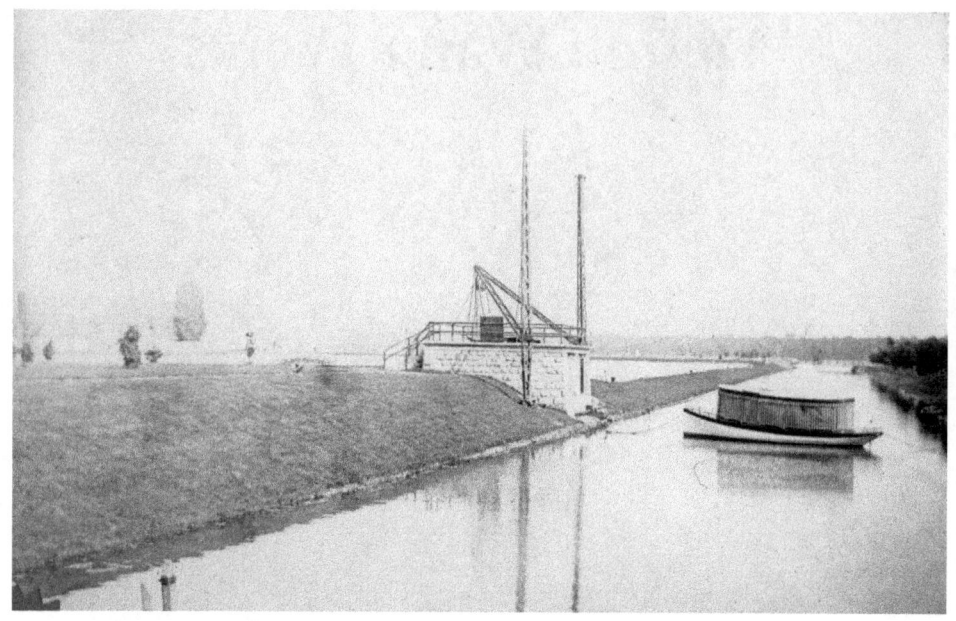

This is an 1897 view of the canal feeding the Detroit Water Works.

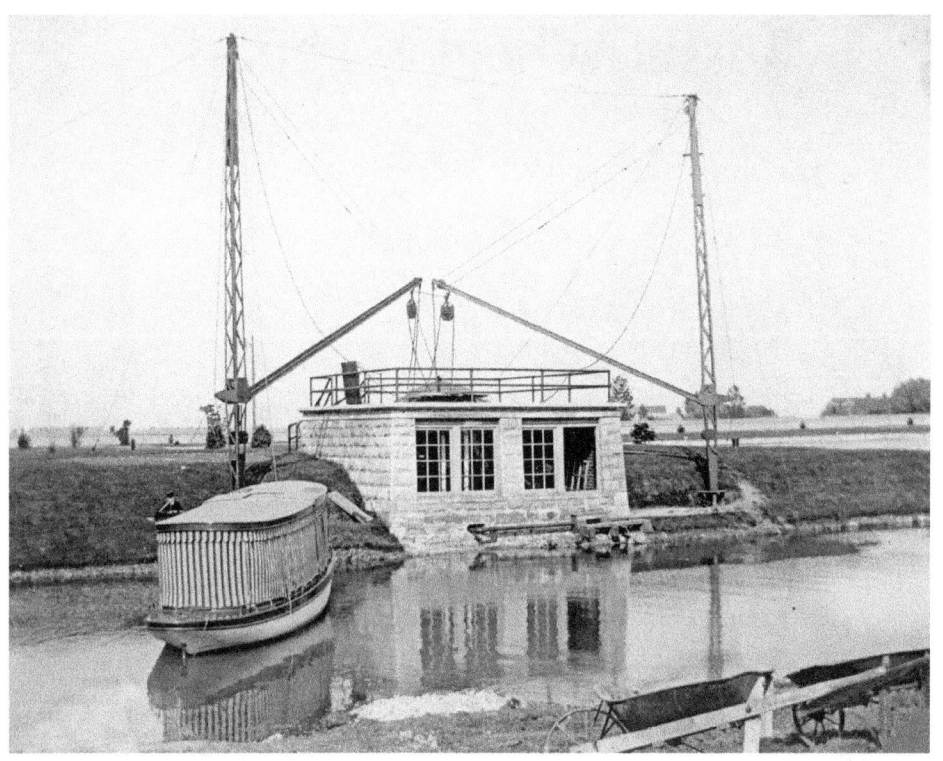

The Detroit Water Works receiving station as it was in 1897.

Russel Wheel & Foundry

A Short History

The Russel Wheel & Foundry Company began operations in a small plant at the foot of Walker Street in either 1876 or 1880. Both dates show up frequently so I am not sure which is correct. I suppose that these dates have been copied incorrectly over and over to the point that the fact has been muddied. They incorporated in January 1883. They manufactured train car wheels and castings. The Pullman Car Company, Lake Shore Railway and Grand Trunk were among its customers.

Russel Wheel & Foundry was the first company to build railroad cars for the sole purpose of moving lumber. These original cars were rigid four-wheel cars and were used by Whitney & Stinchfield in the Saginaw Valley. They carried the logs directly from the logging camp to the sawmill.

As the company grew, they provided the steel structure for buildings and lighthouses. They manufactured the structural steel and assembled it during the construction of the Hammond Building on the corner of Griswold Street and West Fort Street which was torn down and replaced in 1956 by the National Bank of Detroit Building. They also provided the structural steel for the rebuilt Detroit Opera House that was completed in 1898.

In 1892, the Russel Wheel & Foundry purchased about 10 acres along the Central Belt Line where it crossed Joseph Campau Ave. This was very near the home of Francis Ellis.

As the years progressed, they prospered and became one of the largest manufacturing facilities in Detroit. However, when the Great Depression hit, their doors closed forever and those that worked there found themselves unemployed. Among these employees that lost their job was Francis Allen Ellis who had put over thirty years into the company.

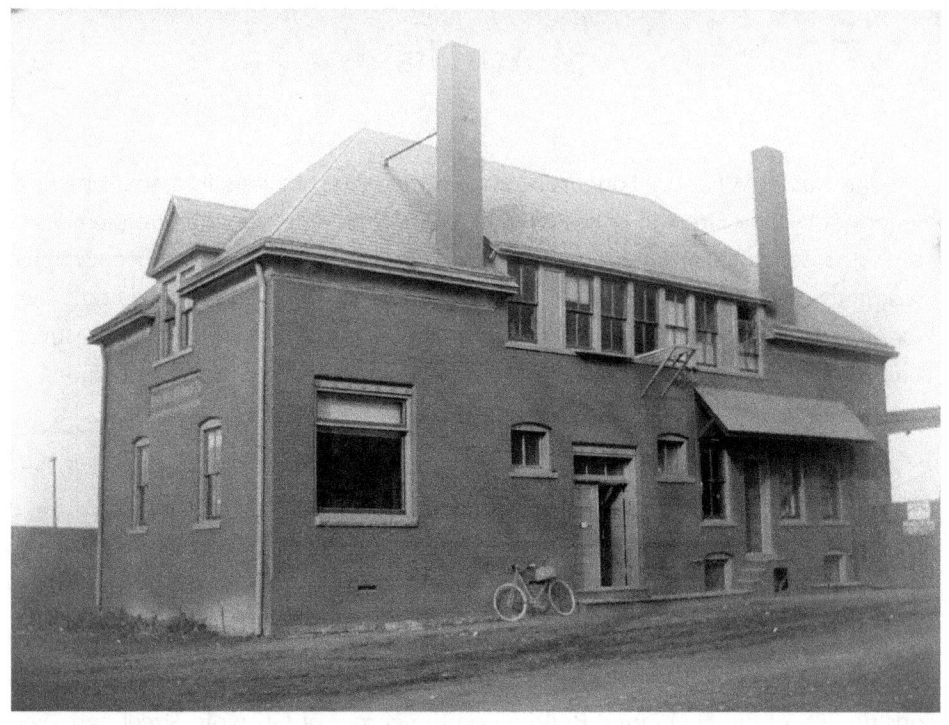

This photo shows the office building where Francis Ellis worked at Russel Wheel & Foundry. His office is on the right side of the building.

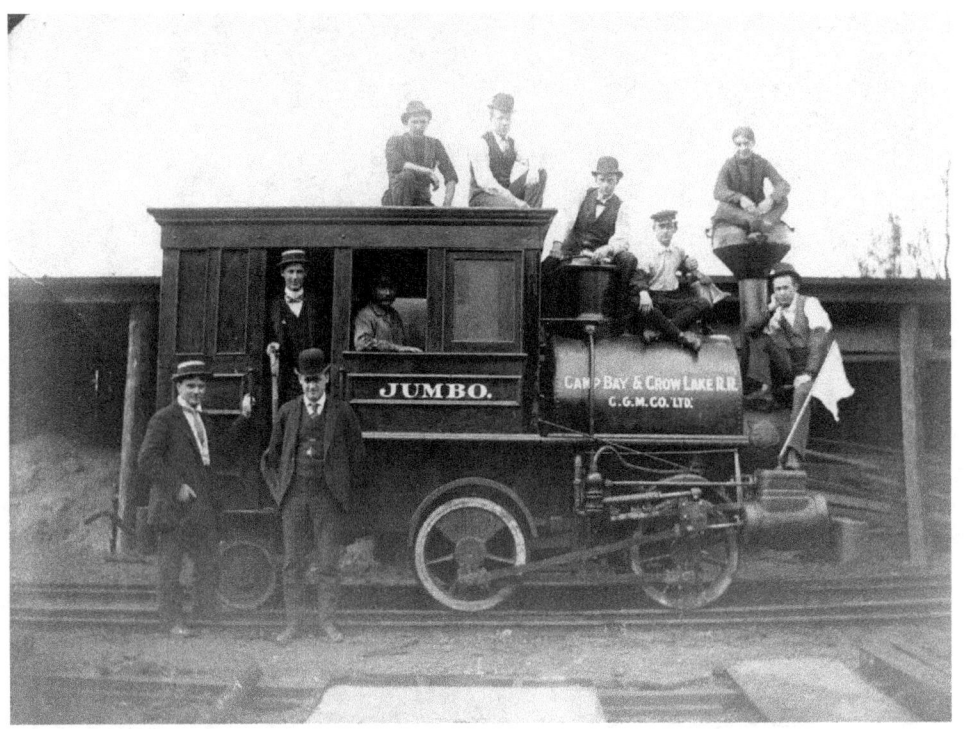

Workers pose for Francis sitting on a Camp Bay & Crow Lake engine.

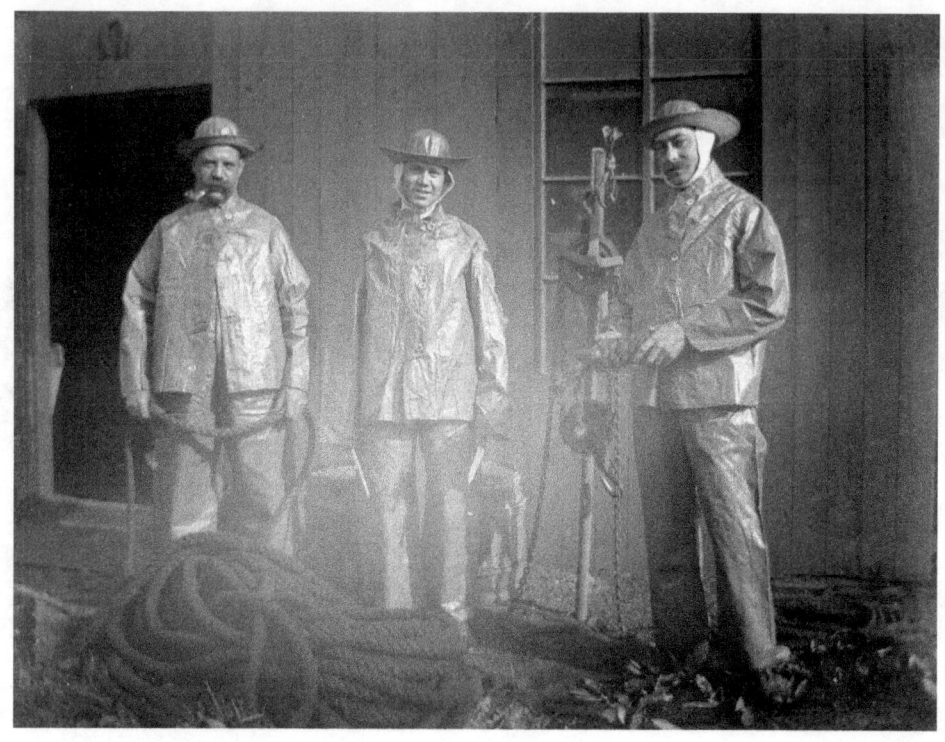

With the task of untangling a rope complete, three workers pose with the coiled rope in front of them. Francis Ellis is in the center.

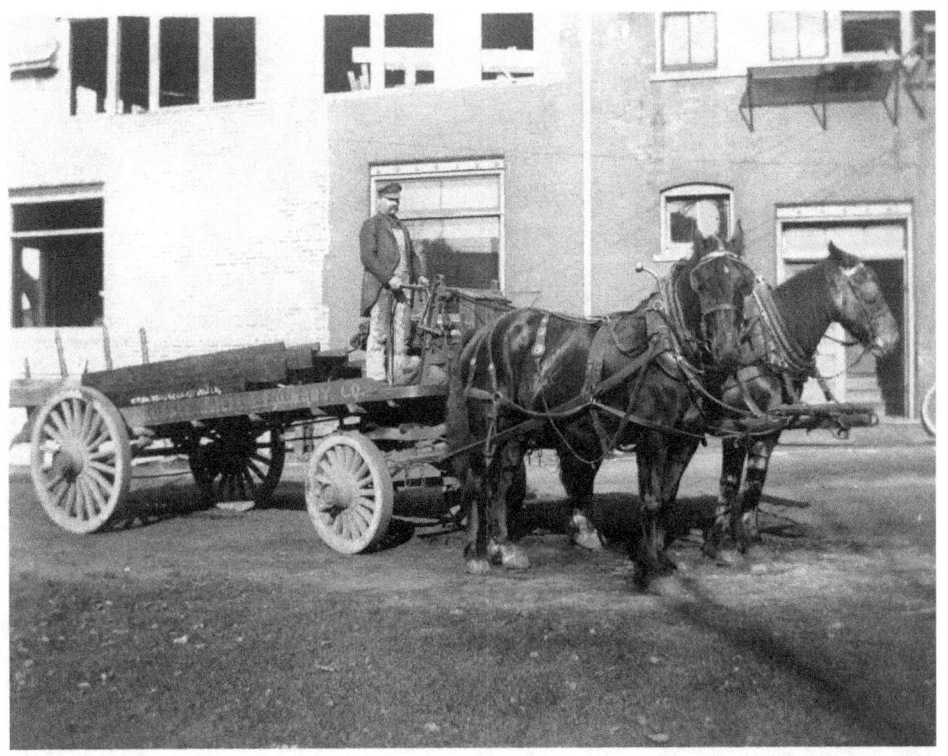

A wagon load of steel beams with the driver holding a pose for the photographer.

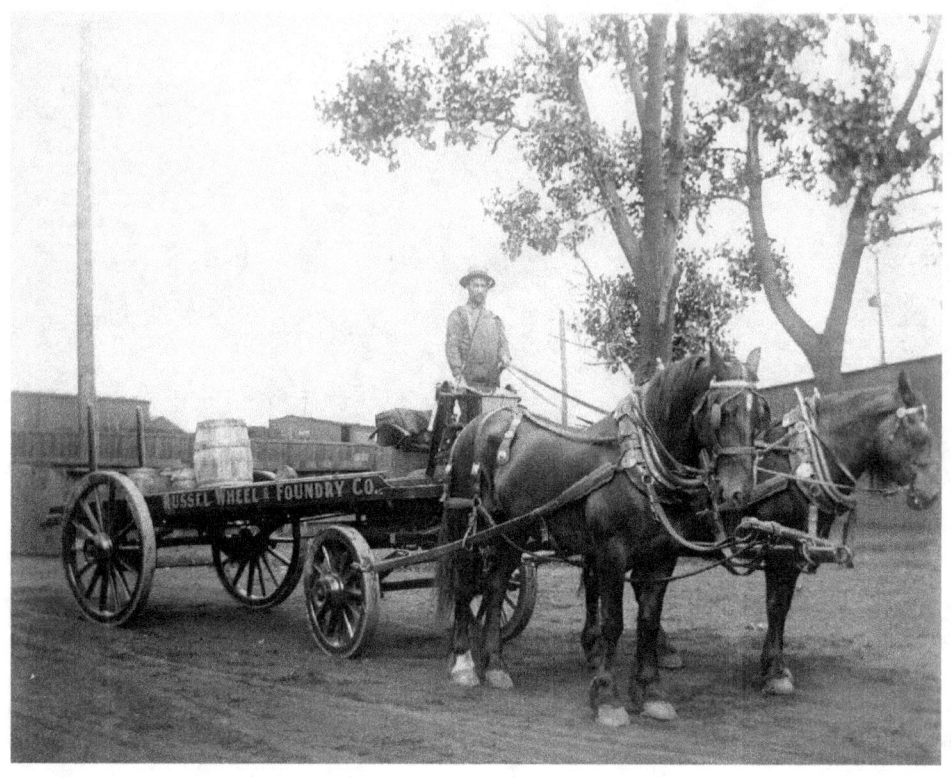

Another wagon stops to pose with a single barrel and some smaller containers.

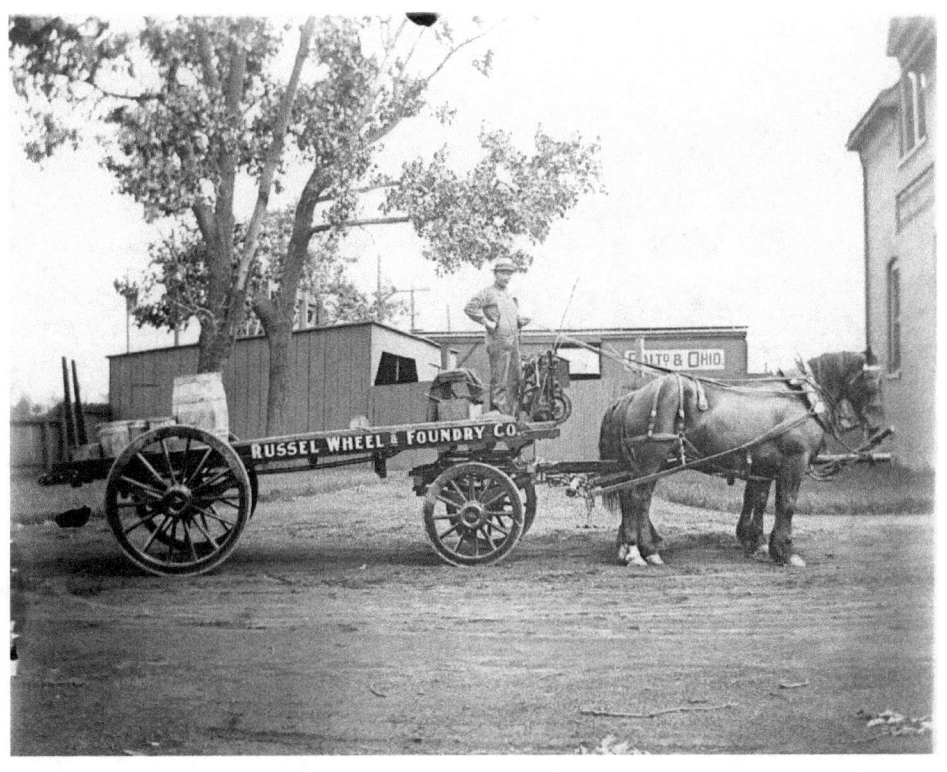

Another view of the same horse drawn wagon holding a barrel.

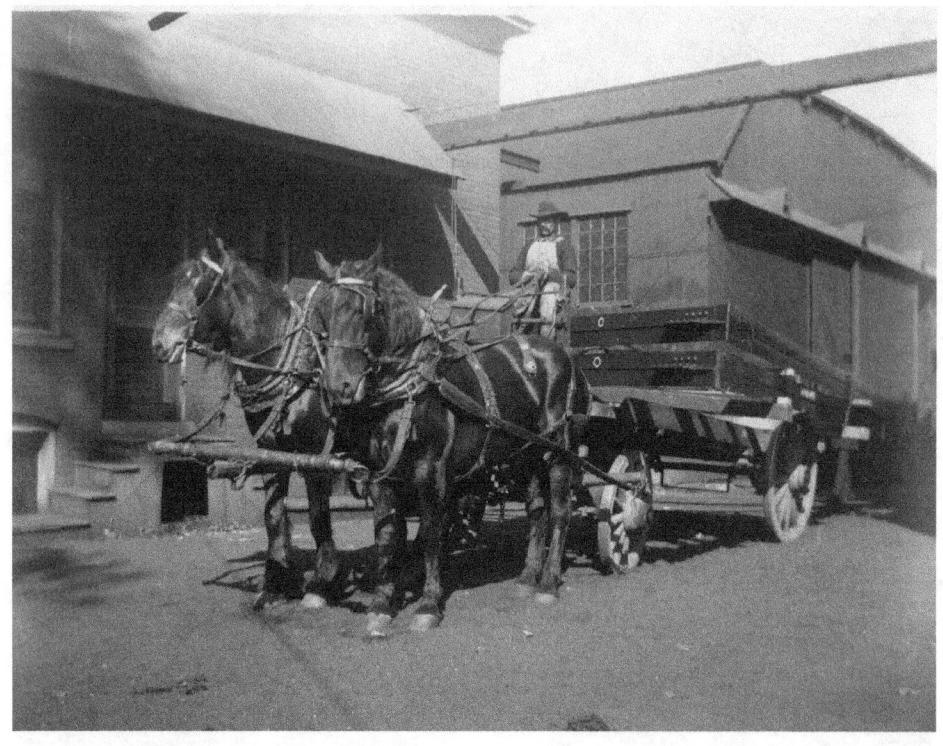

A horse drawn wagon loaded with riveted steel beams at the Russel Wheel & Foundry prepares to deliver its load.

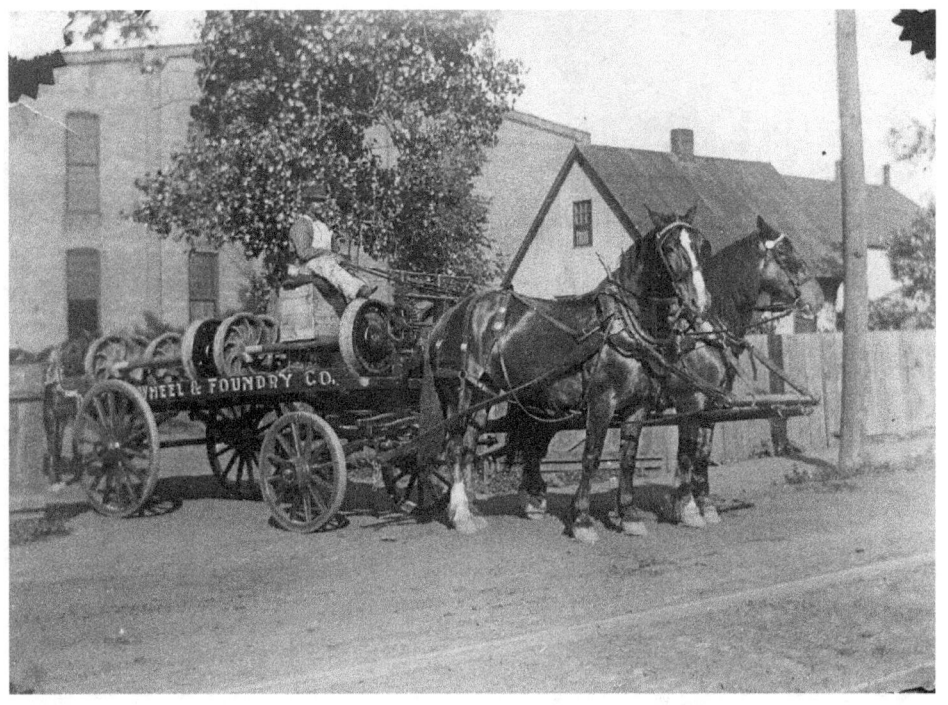

A horse drawn wagon full of train wheels moving on to its next destination.

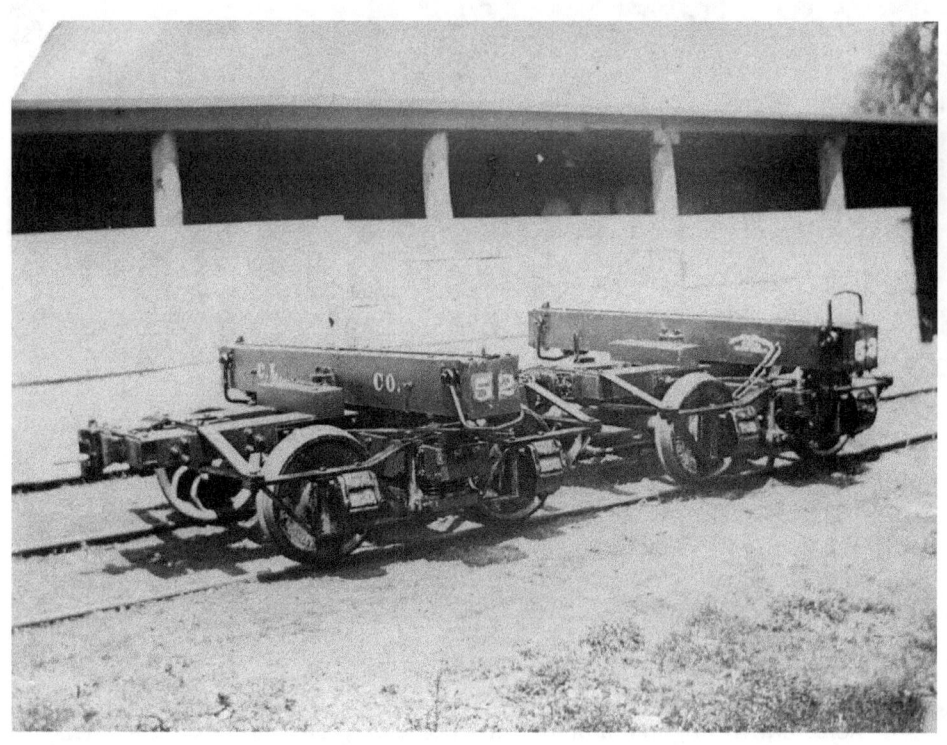

An example of a logging car that the Russel Wheel & Foundry pioneered.

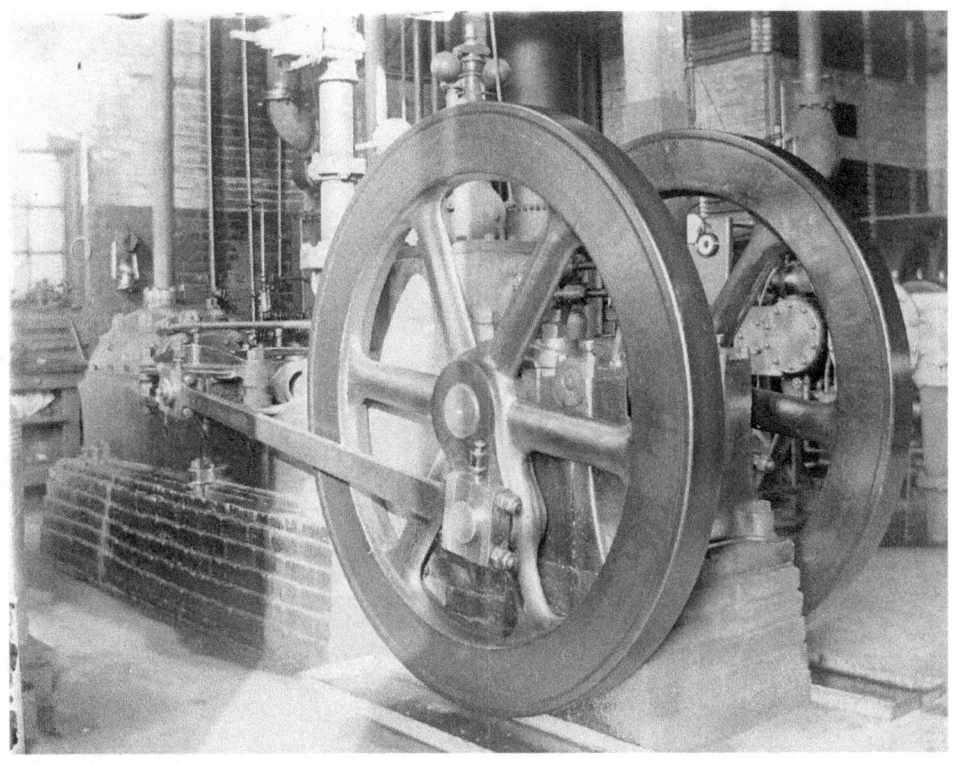

A steam engine sits ready to begin its days run inside the factory. This is one of several views inside the same room.

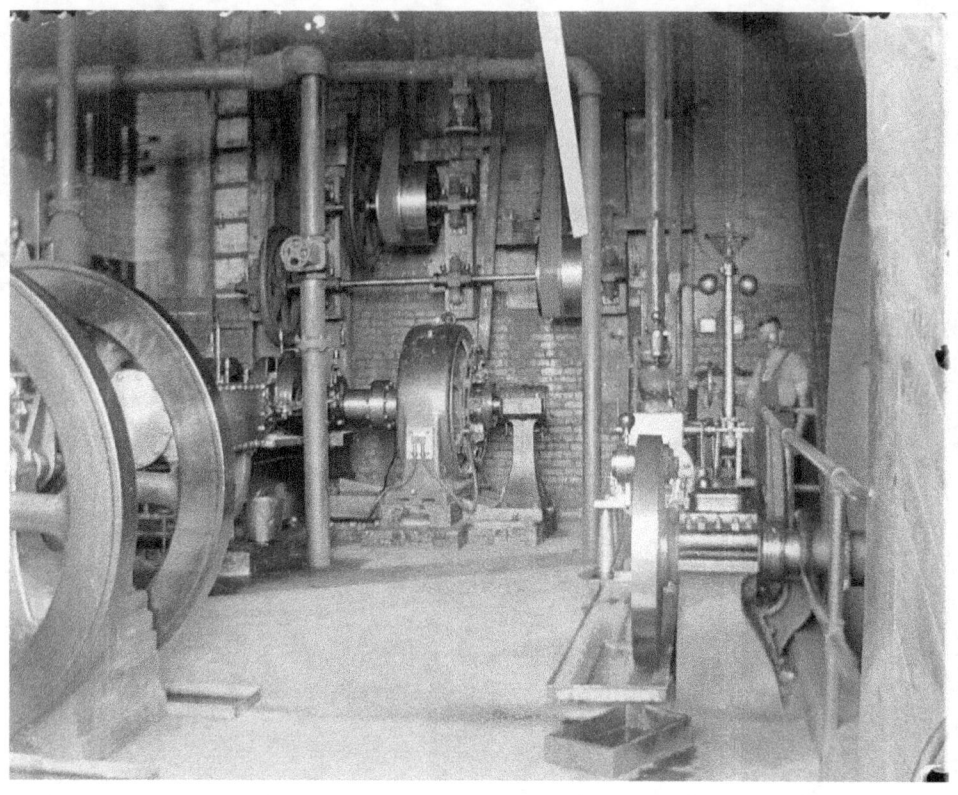

The machinery that the steam engine will drive sits at the ready while a worker prepares for the days work.

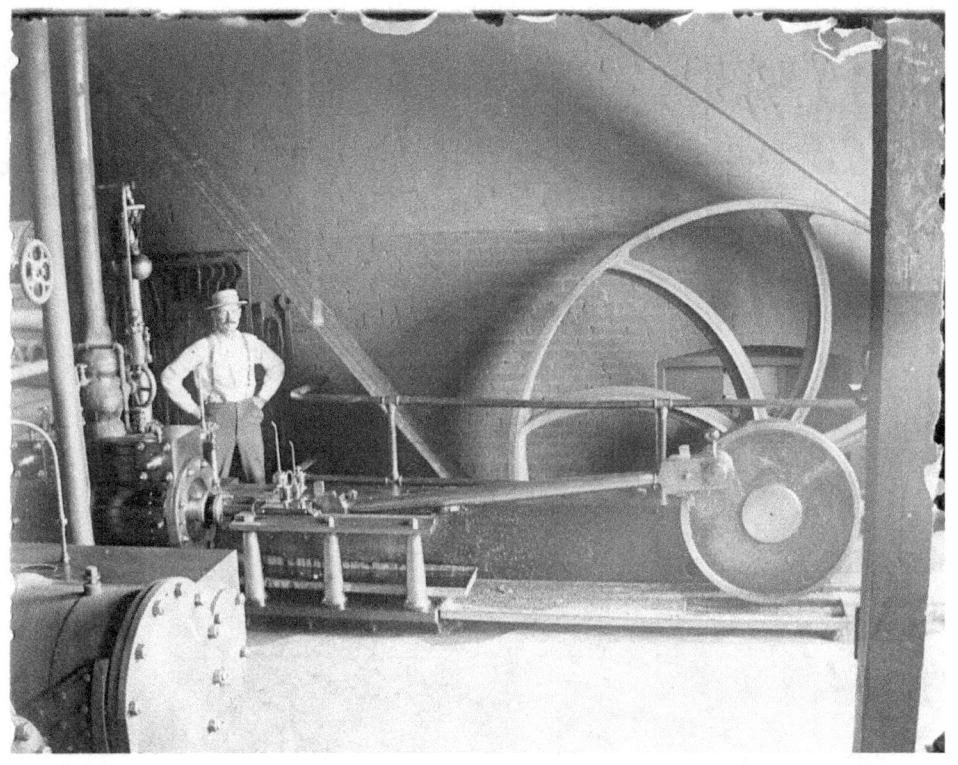

Another worker posing in front of a large drive wheel stands by ready to start his day.

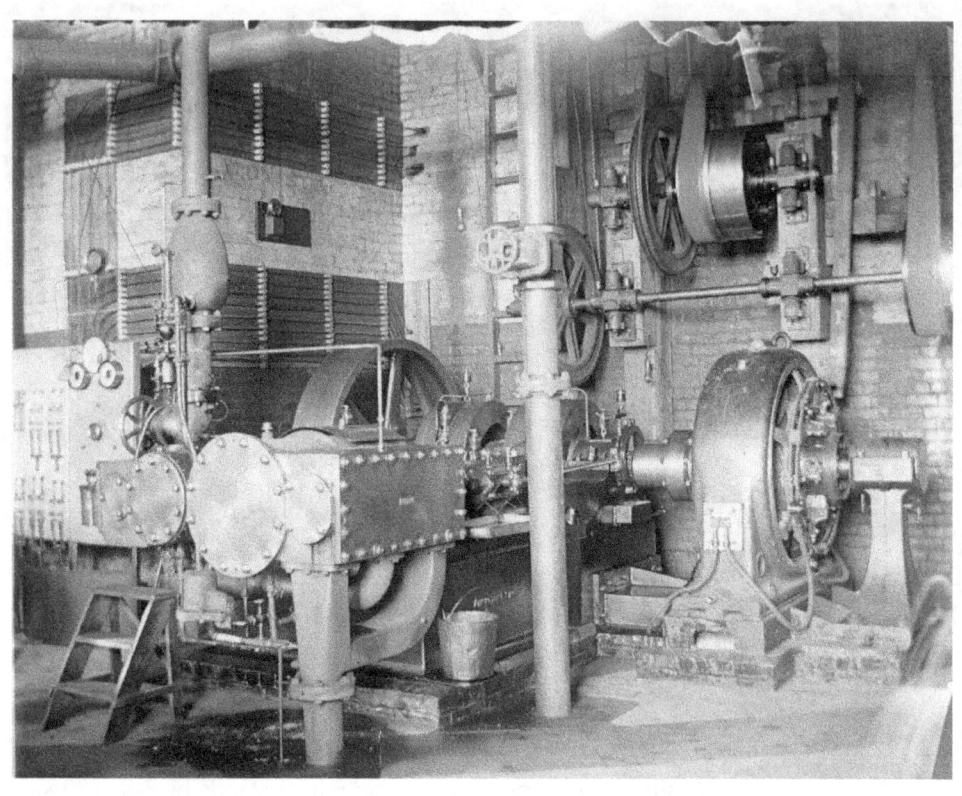

Another view of the mechanical workings inside the factory.

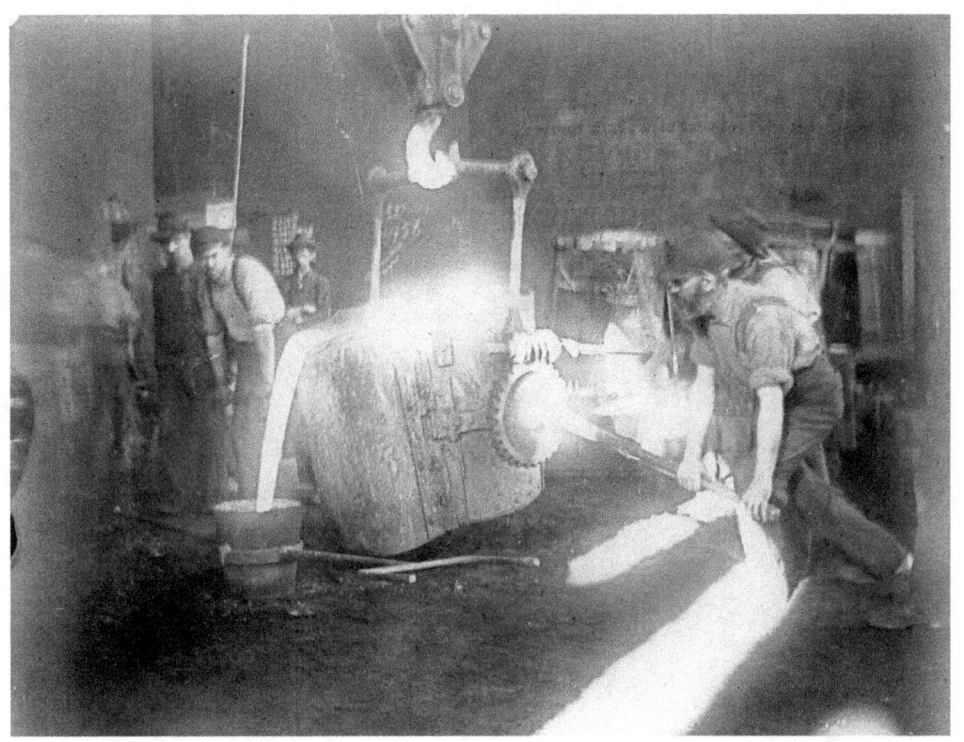

A tough shot to photograph in this time period. Workers pour molten steel into a smaller vessel.

Other Photos

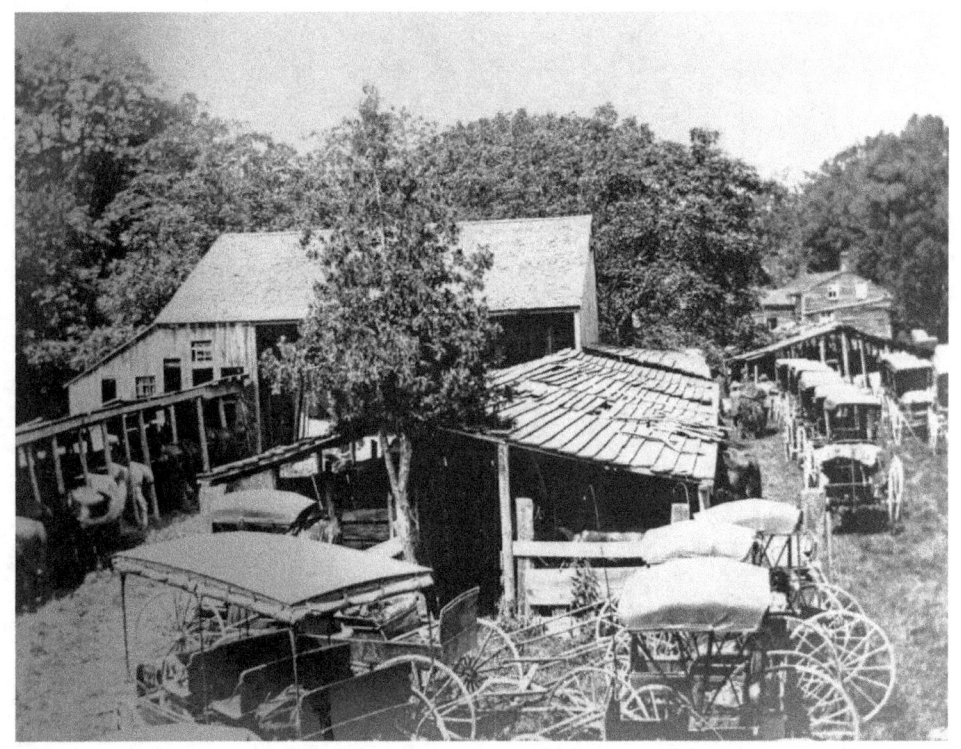

The note left with this photo simply says, "Farmers Picnic." I do not know if this is a Detroit farmers event, but it very well could be.

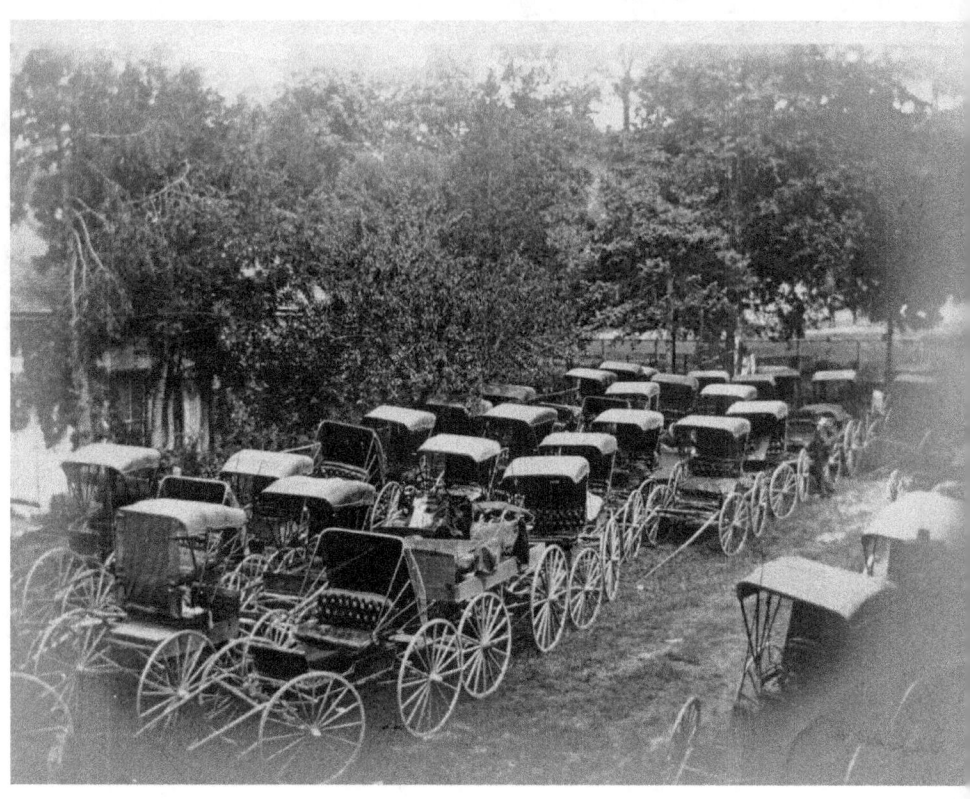

Another view of the parked buggies from the farmers picnic.

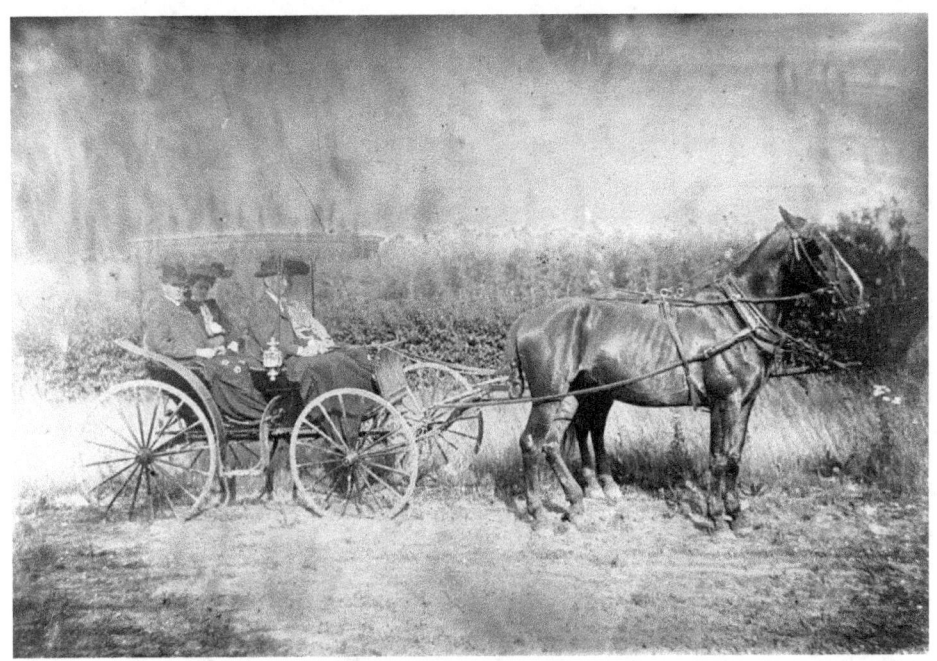

Going for a buggy ride around the turn of the century. Francis Allen Ellis and his wife, Kathryn Belle (Giddings) Ellis, are sitting in the rear. In the front are Kathryn's Uncle Croydon and Aunt Nellie Sutton. The original 5X7 glass plate negative is not in very good condition. I made a direct copy archival negative from which this reproduction was made, and should last at least another 200 years.

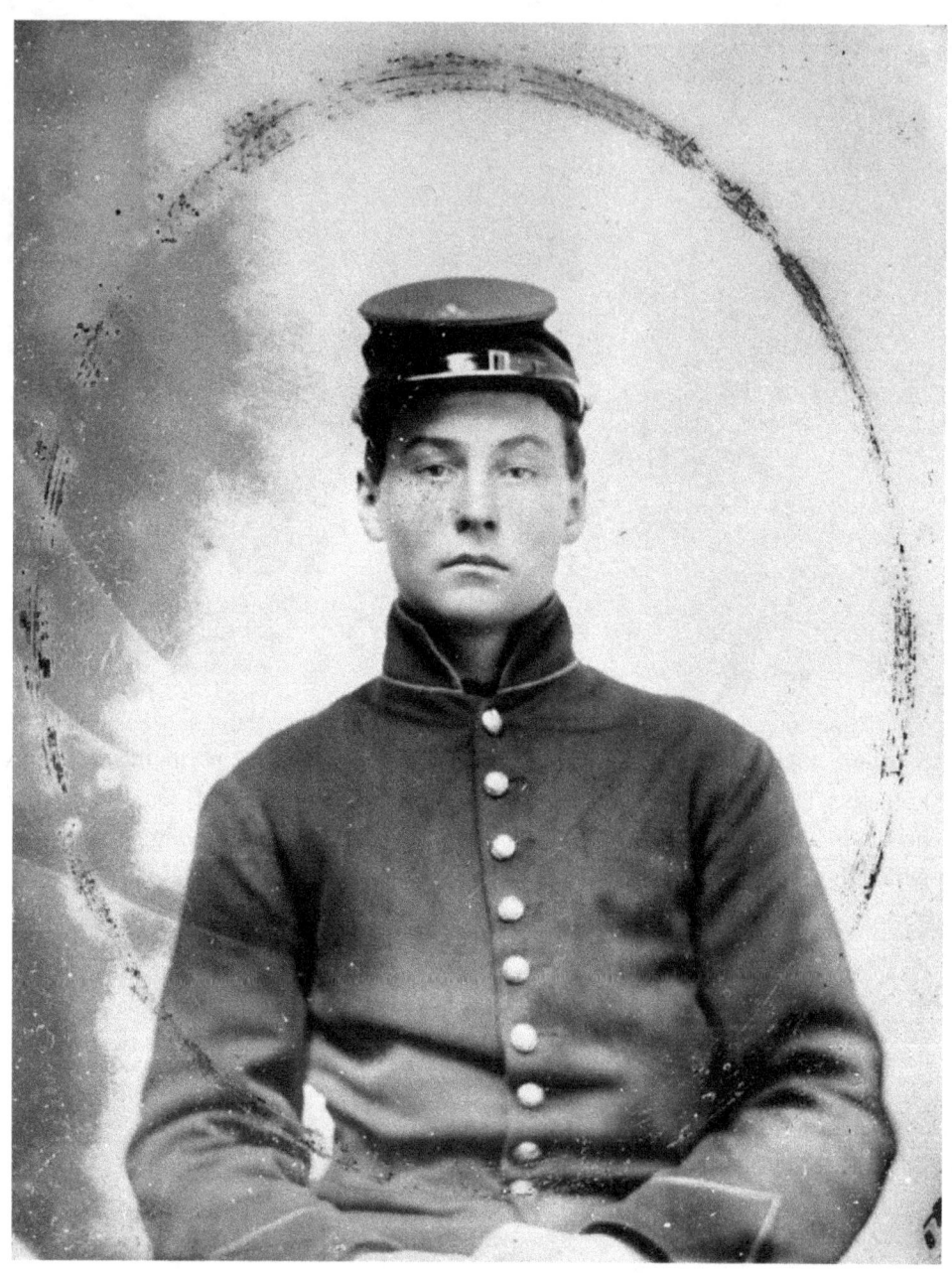

George Abbott Ellis (1844-1896)

My grandfather did not take this photograph but I want to include this great picture of his father, my great grandfather, George Abbott Ellis. George was a veteran of the battle of Gettysburg during the American Civil War. He was a private in the 16th Vermont Volunteer Infantry, Company I. He joined the unit with his brother, Asahel E. Ellis who did not survive the war.

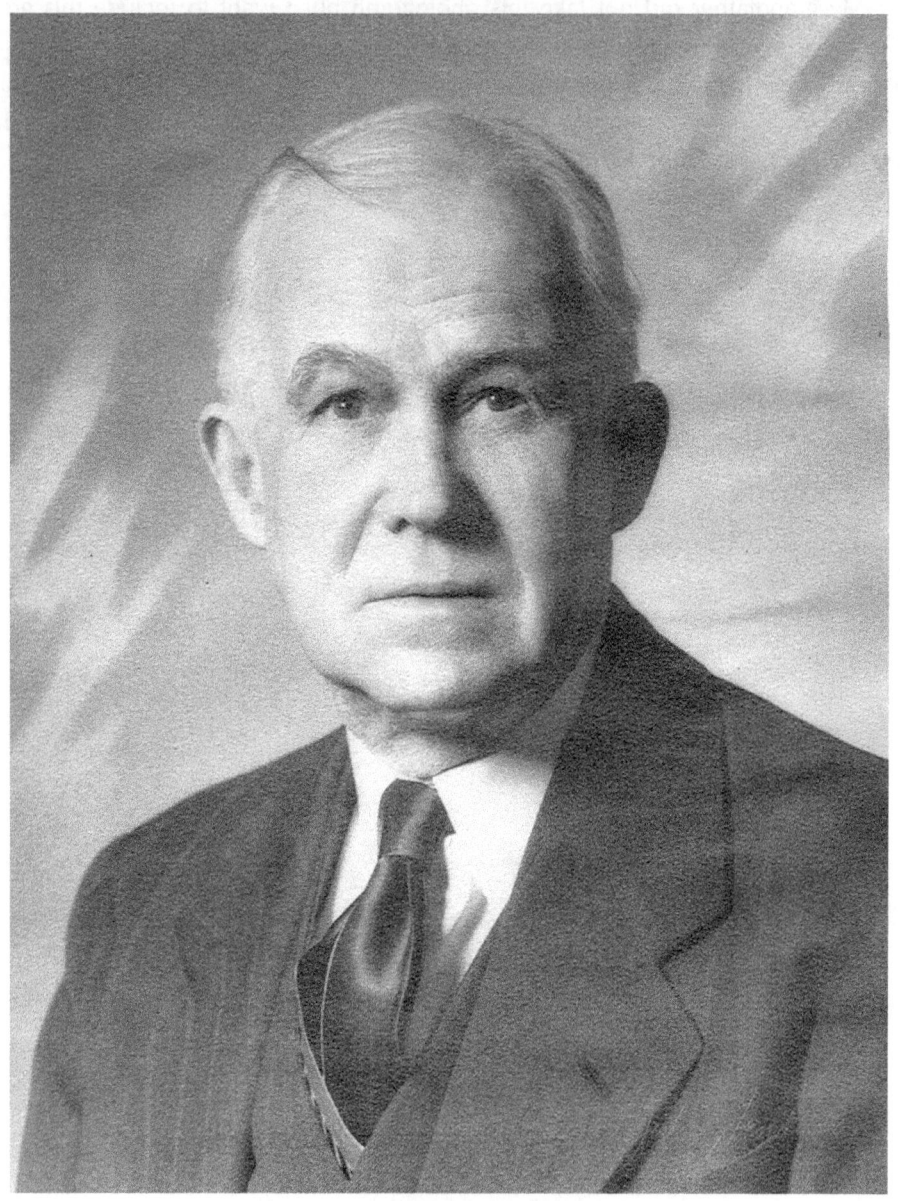

The Photographer
Francis Allen Ellis

About The Author

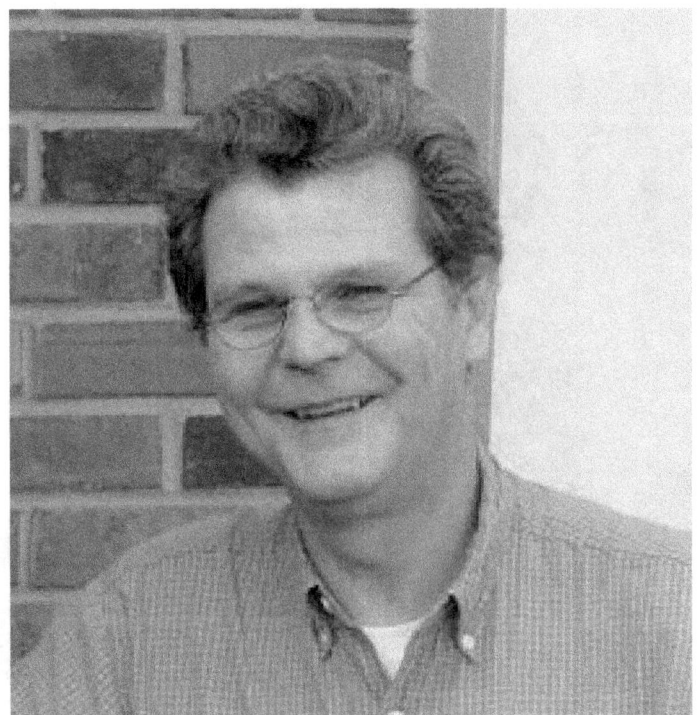

John Francis Ellis lives in Michigan with his wife Sharon and daughter Olivia. His son, Edward, lives in Los Angeles. John was a copyboy at the Detroit Free Press in the early 1970's and has worked as an automotive engineer in the Detroit area for 30 years.

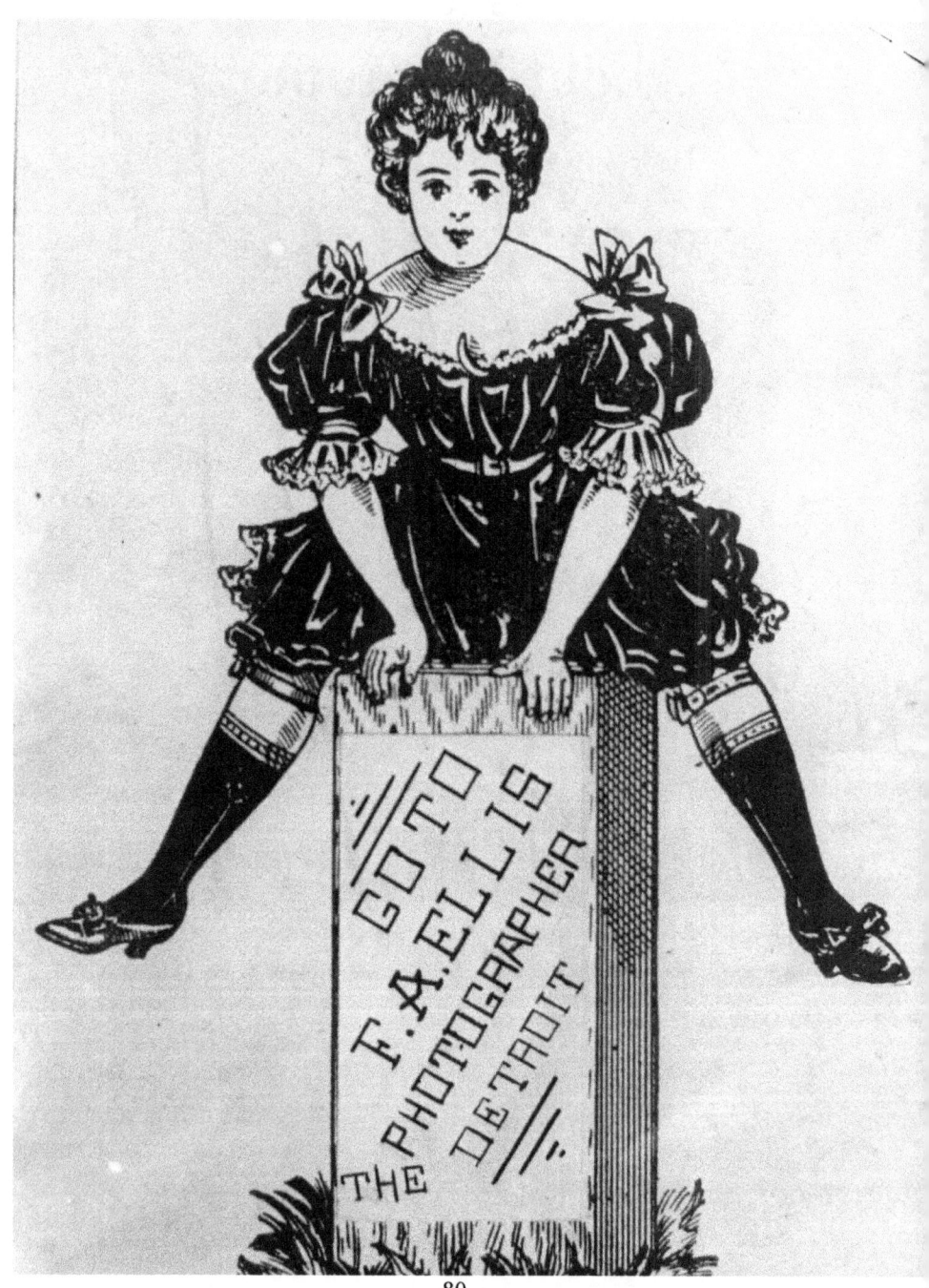

www.ingramcontent.com/pod-product-compliance
Lightning Source LLC
Chambersburg PA
CBHW071613170526
45166CB00003B/1074

* 9 7 8 1 4 8 4 8 9 5 6 5 8 *